USA TODAY'S DEBATE: VOICES AND PERSPECTIVES

LEGALIZING DRUGS

Crime Stopper or Social Risk?

Margaret J. Goldstein

Twenty-First Century Books · Minneapolis

Twenty-First Century Books
A division of Lerner Publishing Group, Inc.
241 First Avenue North
Minneapolis, MN 55401 U.S.A.

Website address: www.lernerbooks.com

The publisher wishes to thank Ben Nussbaum and Phil Pruitt of USA TODAY for their help in preparing this book.

Library of Congress Cataloging-in-Publication Data

Goldstein, Margaret J.
    Legalizing drugs : crime stopper or social risk? / by Margaret J. Goldstein.
        p.   cm. — (USA TODAY's debate: voices and perspectives)
    Includes bibliographical references and index.
    ISBN 978-0-7613-5116-0 (lib. bdg. : alk. paper)
    1. Drug legalization—United States. 2. Drug abuse—Social aspects—United States. I. Title.
HV5825.G5985 2010
364.1'77—dc22   2009024360

Manufactured in the United States of America
1 – DP – 12/15/09

CONTENTS

INTRODUCTION

Crime and Punishment

MICHAEL PHELPS HAS BEEN COMPARED TO A SUPER-hero. Standing 6 feet 4 inches (1.9 meters) tall, the muscled, broad-shouldered swimmer has won sixteen Olympic medals, including a record eight gold medals at a single Olympic Games. He has also racked up world records, world championships, and countless other swimming honors. In the pool, he is remarkably focused. He trains for six hours a day.

Phelps is also remarkably rich due to multimillion-dollar endorsement deals with the Speedo swimsuit company, the Subway sandwich chain, and other corporate sponsors. After he won gold at his first Olympics, the 2004 Games in Athens, Greece, Phelps's picture graced the cover of Wheaties cereal boxes—an honor given to only the top sports champions. After earning eight more gold medals at the 2008 Games in Beijing, China, he appeared on talk shows, awards shows, and magazine covers.

Left: Olympic swimmer Michael Phelps entered into a controversy when he was photographed apparently smoking marijuana.

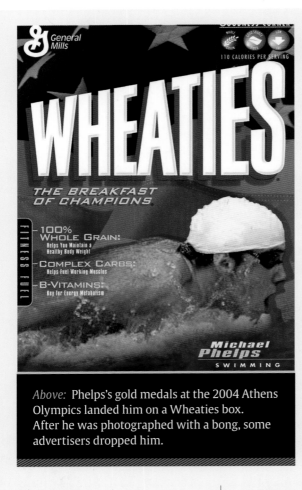

Above: Phelps's gold medals at the 2004 Athens Olympics landed him on a Wheaties box.
After he was photographed with a bong, some advertisers dropped him.

Advertisers love Michael Phelps because he seems like the perfect athlete—disciplined, humble, and wholesome. Parents also love Phelps because he seems like an ideal role model for children. Who wouldn't want their son or daughter to grow up to be just like Michael?

Well, as it turns out, a lot of parents wouldn't—because in early February 2009, Phelps made a bad decision. He was photographed at a party in Columbia, South Carolina, where he was visiting friends. In the picture, he appeared to be smoking from a bong, a water pipe most commonly used for smoking marijuana. The picture appeared in a British newspaper. Back in the United States, the press buzzed about Phelps's transgression. One corporate sponsor, the Kellogg's cereal company, canceled its contract with Phelps. USA Swimming, which oversees competitive swimming in the United States, banned Phelps from competition for three months.

Meanwhile, authorities in Columbia considered whether or not to press charges against Phelps. Possession of marijuana is a crime, with punishment varying by state. Under South Carolina law, Phelps could have gone to jail for up to thirty days had he been arrested and found guilty. Ultimately, the authorities decided not to press charges against Phelps, because the photograph was not sufficient evidence that he had committed a crime. However, the police did arrest eight other partygoers. Seven were charged with marijuana possession and one with selling marijuana.

WHY THE UPROAR?

In some respects, the Michael Phelps marijuana story is not particularly noteworthy. A young man (Phelps was twenty-three at the time) used poor judgment, got caught—at least on camera—and faced the consequences. He wasn't arrested, but he was punished by Kellogg's and USA Swimming. Phelps himself apologized for his actions, saying that he had made a mistake and set a bad example for fans. For some people, that was the end of the story.

For other people, however, the Phelps case was illustrative of a much larger debate. For many years, some people have been arguing that the United States should legalize drugs such as marijuana, cocaine, and heroin. They say that punishing drug users, such as the young people at the party in South Carolina, does more harm than good and that the nation's "War on Drugs" has been a failure. If drugs were legal, some say, the government could control their use. It could tax businesses that sold drugs and make sure that drugs were as safe as possible. Proponents say that legalization could bring all sorts of benefits to U.S. society—everything from decreased crime and terrorism to more money for the U.S. Treasury.

The push for drug legalization is by no means a fringe movement. High-profile leaders, including mayors, governors, police officers, and judges, have endorsed drug legalization and asked Americans to consider it.

But for every American who supports legalization, at least two others oppose it. Opponents of legalization say that legalizing drugs would lead to more drug use, more drug addiction, and more drug-related crime. They say that legalizing drugs would send the wrong message to young people and would encourage them to take drugs.

The U.S. government has passed tough drug laws, and many people think that's a good policy. They believe that society is a much better place with drug users, dealers, and traffickers in jail. They think that the threat of tough punishment will keep kids from experimenting with drugs in the first place.

LOOKING DEEPER

The debate over drug legalization goes beyond pros and cons.

Above: Stephen Jay Gould was a prominent scientist and science writer. Before his death, he used marijuana to relieve nausea caused by cancer treatments. He thought marijuana should be made legal for medical purposes.

> ## " The drug problem is constantly shifting and evolving. "
>
> **—STEVE DNISTRIAN,** EXECUTIVE VICE PRESIDENT,
> PARTNERSHIP FOR A DRUG-FREE AMERICA
>
> **USA TODAY · NOVEMBER 27, 2000**

The debate includes many shades of gray. For instance, some people support legalizing "soft" drugs such as marijuana but not "hard" drugs such as heroin and cocaine. Some people think that both soft and hard drugs should remain illegal but that people who use illegal drugs should go to rehabilitation programs instead of jail. And some point out that the United States already has many dangerous legalized drugs, including tobacco and alcohol.

Clearly, the debate over drug legalization is complicated and controversial. Understanding the debate involves listening to many voices—everyone from high school kids to U.S. presidents. It involves looking at U.S. history and examining drug laws in other countries. Understanding the debate also involves making many predictions and best guesses. Proponents envision a safer, more prosperous, and more peaceful society with drug legalization, while opponents envision a more chaotic and crime-ridden one. Since no one can tell the future, we can't know for sure which side is right. We can only examine the facts and statistics and form our own opinions.

CHAPTER ONE

A History of Drug Use and Abuse

SOME PEOPLE THINK OF DRUG USE AS A MODERN PROBLEM. We often hear about drug abuse in big, crowded cities and crime-ridden neighborhoods. We learn about the modern War on Drugs, in which the U.S. government spends billions of dollars each year to apprehend drug dealers and to prevent drug shipments coming from foreign countries. We hear about drugs in connection to violence, poverty, and illegal activities such as gun smuggling.

Indeed, drug use and abuse are tied to other modern problems. And drug use has increased in recent decades. But drugs are by no means a new phenomenon. In fact, people have most likely been using mind-altering drugs since prehistoric times. Archaeologists think that people in the ancient Americas used drugs derived from peyote cacti and psilocybin mushrooms. People in ancient China and ancient India used marijuana, and people in many ancient societies drank wine and beer.

Historians have found references to opium in the art, literature, and artifacts of many ancient cultures. The famous

Left: This painting from the mid-eighteenth century shows men smoking marijuana in India. In many parts of the world, marijuana use dates to ancient times.

Greek epic poem *The Odyssey* offers this description: "Into the mixing-bowl from which they drank their wine she slipped a drug, heart's-ease, dissolving anger, magic to make us forget our pains. No one who drank it deeply, mulled in wine, could let a tear roll down his cheeks that day." Many scholars think the drug mentioned in this passage is opium.

PHARMACOPOEIA

Drugs and alcohol played varied roles in ancient times. Many people used these substances simply to feel better. The Hebrew Bible or Old Testament, a collection of sacred writings from ancient Israel, advised, "Give strong drink to him who is perishing, and wine to those in bitter distress; let them drink and forget their poverty, and remember their misery no more." Another biblical passage says that God created wine "to gladden the heart of man."

Ancient healers often used drugs as medicine. In China doctors prescribed marijuana tea for malaria, constipation, achy joints, and other health

Below: This Egyptian wall painting from the fourteenth century B.C. shows workers picking grapes and making wine. Drinking alcohol was common in many ancient societies.

problems. Doctors in ancient Greece, Rome, China, and elsewhere prescribed opium for sickness.

In many ancient cultures, drugs played a role in religious practices. In the ancient Americas, for instance, people used peyote and other mind-altering drugs to achieve spiritual visions and to better communicate with their gods. Ancient Jews, Christians, and other groups used wine in their religious ceremonies.

But drug and alcohol use were not always tolerated in ancient times. One manuscript from ancient Egypt describes a priest warning his students, "I, thy superior, forbid thee to go to the taverns. [There] thou art degraded like the beasts." This warning from about 2000 B.C. might be the world's first anti-drug message.

OLD AND NEW WORLDS

Over the centuries, as global travel increased, merchants introduced new drugs into places where they had never been known before. In the late 1400s, European explorers traveled to the Americas by ship. In this "New World," they saw native people smoking the leaves of tobacco plants. Many Europeans were eager to try this drug, which was unknown in Europe. The new European smokers found that tobacco helped them relax. What they didn't know was that the nicotine inside tobacco—the same substance that made smoking pleasurable—was also dangerous and habit forming.

The first permanent English settlement in North America was the Jamestown Colony in Virginia, established in 1607. The Jamestown settlers found that their new home had the perfect soil and climate for tobacco growing. Colonist John Rolfe sent the first shipment of Virginia-grown tobacco to England in 1613. Tobacco quickly became a major industry in the new American colonies.

Back in the "Old World"—in both Europe and the Middle East—smoking tobacco became extremely popular. But some people condemned the activity.

4,000-year-old cave mural in Texas may show peyote ritual

From the Pages of
USA TODAY

A 27-foot [8.2 m] mural painted on a rock wall 4,000 years ago appears to be the oldest depiction of a peyote ritual in the New World, experts say.

The mural, which is called the White Shaman Panel, is in the lower Pecos River region of southwestern Texas. The canyons of the arid region contain hundreds of rock shelters and some of the most dramatic examples of rock art in the world, says Carolyn Boyd, Texas A&M University, College Station.

Peyote is considered a sacred plant by different Native American cultures. It can produce vivid hallucinations. The White Shaman Panel depicts five humanlike figures that extend the length of the panel. Each figure is holding a long, slender black object with red tips. Associated with each figure are X-ray-like or skeletonlike figures and many animallike figures floating behind.

More than 100 black dots are free-floating or superimposed on the figures. An impaled deer is shown with black dots decorating its antlers. At the far left, a humanlike figure holds a weapon and wears deer antlers decorated with black dots on his head. He is superimposed over a large, undulating arch. Running through the length of the mural is a white line that connects each figure. On the far left, the line changes to black.

Previously, archaeologists dismissed the mural as primitive and probably drawn to aid in hunting. Boyd, however, began studying modern rituals among people who claimed ancient ancestry to the region. She also studied other rock art of the area. Boyd says she began to see similarities in style among the rock art of the region—all depicting deer, black dots, arches and skeletonized figures associated with animals.

Boyd found similarities of art style with the modern Huichol Indians of the region, whose belief system ties together peyote, deer and corn into one inseparable sacred symbol. Huichol myths say peyote and rain sprang from the forehead of the deer. Without deer, no peyote and no rain.

In reality, after a rain, deer feast on small bushes beneath which peyote grows, Boyd says. And during an annual ritual, men leave their village and

sojourn single file to find peyote. A shaman leads with a bow and arrow to kill the peyote, which is symbolized by the deer. The men are all connected by a long white cactus fiber that is burned on the end. The black dots represent peyote buttons.

Boyd says she and her colleagues are convinced that the White Shaman Panel depicts a sacred peyote ritual still practiced today.

—Tim Friend

Ancient people in the Americas used mind-altering peyote in religious ceremonies. Some scholars think that rock art in southwestern Texas (above) shows peyote rituals.

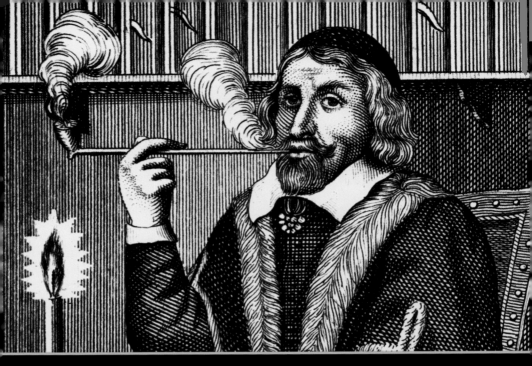

Above: This early nineteenth-century engraving shows sixteenth-century Dutch physician Giles Everard smoking a pipe. Everard believed that tobacco was good medicine.

Church leaders, government officials, and others thought that smoking was a nasty habit. They charged that tobacco smokers became vain and slothful, and they worried that smoking was harmful to human health. Critics also noted the foul smell of tobacco smoke and the potential for careless smokers to start fires.

In various cities in Russia, western Europe, and the Middle East, authorities outlawed smoking. In some places, penalties for breaking the law were severe, including beheading and hanging. But the laws didn't work. Europeans and Middle Easterners continued to smoke, despite the threat of punishment.

People also continued to drink alcohol and use other mind-altering drugs. Opium use was particularly common. In the 1700s, people in Great Britain and North America could buy opium-based treatments at apothecary shops, or pharmacies. The remedies—sold as tinctures, syrups, powders, and lozenges—were touted to treat everything from insomnia to smallpox. Even if the medicines didn't succeed in curing diseases, they usually made the sufferer feel better—at least temporarily.

TEMPERANCE AND TOLERANCE

In the late eighteenth century, colonists in North America fought a war for independence (1775–1783) and created the United States of America. Drinking was widespread in the new nation, in part because water supplies were often contaminated with disease-carrying organisms. Beer and wine were safer to drink than water.

A few U.S. leaders condemned drunkenness and hoped to have drinking curtailed. In the 1790s, Benjamin Rush, a leading physician and politician, advised Congress to impose high taxes on distilled liquor, such as gin, rum, and whiskey, as a way to discourage drinking. Gradually, more Americans took the same view. Around 1800, Americans started to form temperance societies—groups that wanted to outlaw alcoholic beverages. Society members believed that drunkenness led to sickness, crime, poverty, and misery. They noted that workingmen often spent their wages on drink instead of using them to care for their families.

Few people sounded the alarm about other drugs in the nineteenth century, however. Americans still bought opium-based remedies at pharmacies. They also bought marijuana to treat headaches, muscle aches, and insomnia. Early in the century, scientists identified morphine, the active ingredient in opium and a powerful painkiller. The drug was particularly effective in relieving the suffering of soldiers wounded in the Civil War (1861–1865). Cocaine, which comes from the leaves of the coca plant, arrived in the United States in the late 1800s. Doctors prescribed it to treat all sorts of mental and physical ailments.

The United States had few laws to regulate the sale or use of such drugs, and doctors then did not think the drugs were dangerous. Americans used the drugs legally and liberally, with or without a doctor's prescription. Many store-bought remedies—such as Mrs. Winslow's Soothing Syrup (for children) and Colwell's Egyptian Oil—contained opium or morphine. In Atlanta, Georgia, pharmacist John Pemberton invented Coca-Cola in 1886. The label on the bottle said that Coca-Cola was "a valuable brain tonic, and a cure for all nervous affections—sick headache, neuralgia, hysteria, melancholy." What the label didn't reveal was that the popular new soft drink contained cocaine. Heroin, derived from morphine, also came on the market around this time. Doctors dispensed it freely for pain and other afflictions.

CRACKDOWN

Morphine, cocaine, and other drugs were clearly taking their toll. Some people used them only occasionally and with few ill effects. But other Americans, when under the influence of such drugs, neglected their work, their health, and their families. The drugs

Above: This advertisement for Mrs. Winslow's Soothing Syrup appeared in 1888. The remedy contained morphine.

were addictive, meaning that people physically craved them and often needed higher and higher doses to feel their effects. One historian estimates that during the 1890s, more than three hundred thousand Americans were addicted to opiates (drugs derived from opium).

these unfortunates the precious promise of eternal life."

Government leaders, too, grew concerned about drug use. In the early twentieth century, they passed the first in a long series of drug laws. The Pure Food and Drug Act of 1906 required manufacturers to list

> ## " Cocaine Toothache Drops, Instantaneous Cure! Price 15 Cents. "
>
> —LLOYD MANUFACTURING CO. ADVERTISEMENT FOR TOOTHACHE REMEDY, LATE NINETEENTH CENTURY

The authorities began to take notice. U.S. doctors realized that morphine and other opiates were not merely harmless painkillers to be dispensed liberally. They called for laws to restrict the sale and use of addictive drugs. One physician, John Witherspoon, urged his fellow doctors to "save our people from the clutches of this hydra-headed monster [opium] which stalks abroad throughout the civilized world, wrecking lives and happy homes, filling our jails and lunatic asylums, and taking from

the drugs contained in their medicines on product labels. The Harrison Narcotics Act of 1914 taxed and regulated the sale of opiates and cocaine. The 1924 Heroin Act made it illegal to manufacture heroin. These laws effectively eliminated drugs in store-bought products, although doctors could still prescribe opiates to patients. Drugs became harder to get, but many people still used them. Some bought drugs on the black market—a network of illegal buying and selling.

The Opium Wars

For thousands of years, people in China used opium freely, just as people did in Europe and other places. And as in other places, opium use took a heavy toll in China. Some people became addicted to the drug. They neglected their work and families. Their health suffered.

In the 1700s, merchants from Great Britain and North America found they could make big profits by selling opium in China. The opium came from British-controlled India. But the Chinese government, alarmed about the growing number of Chinese addicts, wanted to stop the opium trade. In the late 1700s, China outlawed the sale and importation of opium. This legislation did not stop the opium merchants, however. They continued to smuggle the drug into China illegally.

In 1839 the Chinese again tried to stop the opium trade. This time Chinese officials seized a giant shipment of opium from British merchants. For many years, relations between China and Great Britain had been tense. The seizure of the British opium

Above: British ships bombard Canton (Guangzhou), China, during the First Opium War.

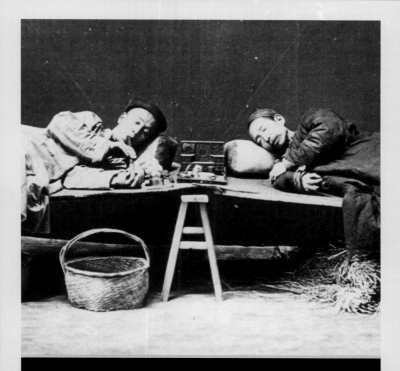

Above: This photograph from the 1870s shows Chinese men smoking opium.

served as a spark that led to the First Opium War. The war ended in 1842 with a Chinese defeat. The peace treaty that followed gave a number of political and economic rewards to Great Britain, including the right to keep selling opium in China. The British also forced China to sign similar treaties with France and the United States.

A Second Opium War between China and Britain occurred in 1856. The British again defeated the Chinese and forced additional trade concessions. The opium trade continued for many more years, and many Chinese people continued to suffer the ill effects of opium addiction.

DEMON RUM

The movement to control narcotics was far overshadowed in this era by the movement to outlaw alcohol. By the early twentieth century, the temperance movement had grown into a powerful national force. Groups such as the Prohibition Party, the Woman's Christian Temperance Union, and the Anti-Saloon League had gathered millions of members and considerable political clout. Temperance leaders preached that liquor was a threat to youth, home, family, and prosperity. They were convinced that a nationwide prohibition, or ban, on alcohol would cleanse the United States of a variety of social ills.

Above: Carry Nation, known as the Kansas Saloon Smasher, was well known in the temperance movement of the late nineteenth century.

One by one, U.S. states began to "go dry"—outlawing the manufacture and sale of alcohol within state borders. Meanwhile, temperance leaders pushed for a constitutional amendment that would extend Prohibition to the entire nation.

By 1916 Prohibition forces were perched on the edge of victory. Twenty-six states had gone dry, and many others were considering dry laws. The next year, the United States entered World War I (1914–1918). This war in Europe gave Prohibition forces the final push they needed for a nationwide ban. The Prohibitionists charged that alcohol sapped the strength and determination of U.S. soldiers. They argued further that the United States shouldn't be using grains to make whiskey and beer when U.S. troops and their overseas fighting partners desperately needed food. The traffic in liquor was "un-American . . . crime-producing, food-wasting, youth-corrupting, [and] home-wrecking," argued the Prohibitionists. They succeeded in making Prohibition seem patriotic.

Many Americans opposed Prohibition. These opponents included brewers and liquor manufacturers, as well as many people who simply enjoyed an occasional drink. But the Prohibition forces were far stronger and more vocal. In late 1917, Congress passed the Eighteenth Amendment to the U.S. Constitution, which banned the sale, manufacture, transportation, import, and export of "intoxicating liquors." The states ratified the amendment a little over a year later.

LAW OF THE LAND

Prohibition took effect in January 1920. To comply with the law, breweries and distilleries shut down or switched to manufacturing legal beverages. Stores stopped selling alcohol, and restaurants stopped serving it. Many Americans immediately quit drinking simply because liquor was no longer readily available. Others did so to obey the new law. But many Americans still wanted to buy

> " **The saloon is the most fiendish, corrupt, hell-soaked institution that ever crawled out of the slime of the eternal pit.** "

—PROHIBITIONIST PREACHER MARK MATTHEWS, SEATTLE, WASHINGTON, 1910s liquor, and if they couldn't do so legally, they would do so illegally.

A network quickly arose to supply those who wanted alcohol. Smugglers sneaked in liquor from Europe, the West Indies, and Canada. People also cooked homemade batches of "bathtub gin" and moonshine (some of it poisonous). In cities, people drank at illegal night-clubs called speakeasies. New York City alone had an esti-mated thirty thousand speak-easies by 1927.

Selling liquor became big business, with vast profits for those willing to break the law. Criminal gangs, armed with machine guns and led by men such as Al Capone, fought one another to control the liquor trade. Understaffed and under-funded, the U.S. Prohibition Bureau could not keep pace with the lawbreakers. Making matters worse, many police officers, judges, politicians, and even Prohibition agents took bribes from bootleggers (people who dealt in illegal liquor). The

Above: A federal agent destroys barrels of illegal liquor during the 1920s. Agents had a hard time fighting smugglers during Prohibition.

> **We should have learned from Prohibition how foolish it is to hand huge chunks of our economy to black marketers who will not hesitate to use the money and distribution channels for other, more serious crimes.**
>
> —COLUMNIST PATRICK COX
> **USA TODAY** · OCTOBER 15, 2002

officials allowed the illegal dealings to go forward in exchange for a cut of the profits.

By the late 1920s, many Americans were convinced that Prohibition was causing more harm than good. The law led to crime and violence, opponents said, and some people were drinking more than ever before. In 1929 the U.S. stock market crashed, plunging the nation into the Great Depression (1929–1942). Millions of Americans lost their jobs. The Depression gave more fuel to the anti-Prohibition forces. They argued that a legal liquor industry would help revive the economy by creating jobs and providing badly needed tax revenues to government.

By 1932, when Franklin D. Roosevelt had won the presidency, the nation was at last ready to change the Prohibition law. In early 1933, Congress passed the Twenty-First Amendment, which repealed (legally did away with) Prohibition, and the states quickly ratified it.

The liquor business underwent a quick transformation. Legal breweries and distilleries started up again. Stores and restaurants once again served legal liquor to paying customers. Some of the gangsters and bootleggers who had operated outside the law during Prohibition became legitimate liquor dealers afterward.

CHAPTER TWO

The War on Drugs

As PROHIBITION WAS NEARING ITS END, U.S. OFFICIALS turned their attention back to drug control. In 1930 the federal government combined two agencies, the Bureau of Prohibition and the Federal Narcotics Control Board, to create the Federal Bureau of Narcotics. This agency was in charge of overseeing U.S. drug control and enforcement. At its head was Harry J. Anslinger, a former Prohibition official and a fierce antidrug crusader.

KILLER WEED

Under Anslinger's leadership, the Federal Bureau of Narcotics cast a critical eye on marijuana, a drug derived from the hemp plant. Like opium, this drug had long been used as medicine in the United States and elsewhere. But Anslinger saw a negative side to marijuana, which he termed a "killer weed." Marijuana use was not widespread in this era. Most middle-class Americans had barely even heard of the drug. But in the 1930s, the Federal Bureau of Narcotics set out to

Left: Harry J. Anslinger headed the Federal Bureau of Narcotics from 1930 until 1962.

teach the nation about its dangers via pamphlets, books, and educational films. One 1936 Narcotics Bureau pamphlet warned:

> Prolonged use of marihuana frequently develops a delirious rage which sometimes leads to high crimes such as assault and murder. Hence marihuana has been called the "killer drug." The habitual use of this narcotic poison always causes a very marked mental deterioration and sometimes produces insanity. Hence marihuana is frequently called "loco weed."

Anslinger fought to have marijuana criminalized at both the state and federal levels, and he successfully ushered in the 1937 Marijuana Tax Act. This law effectively outlawed marijuana by making it subject to extremely high taxes and strict licensing requirements.

Not everyone was convinced that marijuana was as harmful as Anslinger claimed it was, however. In 1939 the New York Academy of Medicine conducted a study of marijuana's medical and social effects. The academy's report, issued in 1944, called marijuana a "mild, nonaddictive euphoriant" with no direct links to physical health problems, mental health problems, crime, or societal decay. This report did little to sway the opinions of Anslinger and other government officials, however. Marijuana remained on the list of illegal drugs, alongside cocaine, heroin, and other narcotics.

TURN ON, TUNE IN, DROP OUT

For the most part, drug use in the mid-twentieth century remained in the shadows. Although many Americans had sneaked illegal liquor during Prohibition, they were far more law abiding when it came to drugs such as marijuana and heroin. Generally, drug users were on the margins of society. For instance, some African American jazz musicians experimented with heroin. A small group of writers and artists—the so-called beatniks of the 1950s—also used mind-altering drugs. But most mainstream white Americans rarely encountered drugs.

Playing the Race Card

The early fight against drug use in the United States often took on a racist cast. Officials singled out specific racial and ethnic groups, linked them to drug use, and then played on people's prejudices to condemn both the drug and the user. For example, in 1914 the *New York Times* printed an article with the inflammatory headline "Negro Cocaine 'Fiends' Are a New Southern Menace." A doctor in Philadelphia similarly claimed, "Most of the attacks upon white women of the South are the direct result of the cocaine-crazed Negro brain." Such statements capitalized upon the fears and racial prejudices of white Americans, convincing them that cocaine was a sinister drug that had to be outlawed.

The Prohibitionists used a related tactic to convince people that alcohol should be banned in the 1910s. In that decade, the United States fought in World War I. The main U.S. enemy in the war was Germany, and distrust of German Americans ran high across the United States. Since much of the beer produced in the United States came from breweries owned by German Americans, the Prohibitionists were able to demonize alcohol and Germans all at the same time. Wayne Wheeler of the Anti-Saloon League noted that the "Anheuser-Busch Company and some of the Milwaukee [brewing] companies are largely controlled by alien Germans." He called these businesses "alien enemies" and asked Attorney General A. Mitchell Palmer to investigate them for anti-American activities.

The demonization of marijuana in the 1930s took on blatantly racist tones. In testimony before Congress in 1937, Harry Anslinger of the Federal Bureau of Narcotics neatly combined drug use, racial minorities, "satanic" jazz music, and then-taboo interracial relationships into one frightening package. "Most marijuana smokers are Negroes, Hispanics, Filipinos and entertainers," Anslinger declared. "Their satanic music, jazz and swing result from marijuana usage. This marijuana causes white women to seek sexual relations with Negroes." Such incendiary language successfully convinced the nation that marijuana was a menace that needed to be destroyed.

Change came in the 1960s. Although older Americans of this decade tended to be conservative, family oriented, religious, and respectful of authority, the younger generation made an abrupt transformation in the early 1960s. A youth rebellion swept the nation. Young people—especially on college campuses—began to protest against U.S. involvement in the Vietnam War (1957–1975). They questioned the long-standing traditions of U.S. government and business, and they rejected the social norms of their parents. Hippies—as the young rebels were called—listened to rock-and-roll music, dressed in colorful flowing clothing, and experimented with drugs.

Above: Two hippies smoke marijuana at Golden Gate Park in San Francisco. Many young people experimented with drugs in the 1960s.

At first, marijuana was the hippie drug of choice. It became a symbol of the new counterculture. But young people also experimented with other, stronger drugs, such as hashish (which, like marijuana, is derived from hemp), psilocybin mushrooms, and lysergic acid diethylamide (LSD).

No longer relegated to the fringes of society, drug use took center stage among white, middle-class, college-educated youths. Some people even praised drugs for their mind-expanding properties. For instance, psychologist Timothy Leary advised young people to "turn on, tune in, and drop out"— that is, to reject social norms and find spiritual meaning through drug use. Many artists and musicians made strange, vibrant, and dreamlike creations under the influence of drugs. But in several cases, drug use led to tragedy. For instance, talented blues singer Janis Joplin, only twenty-seven years old, died in 1970 of a heroin overdose.

The social turmoil of the era spilled across society as a whole. As it did, drug use increased— not just on college campuses but also in high schools, poor inner-city neighborhoods, and among U.S. troops fighting in Vietnam. Not surprisingly, parents, teachers, community leaders, and government officials became alarmed. "The heroin addiction crisis has reached threatening proportions," proclaimed Florida Congressman Claude Pepper in 1971. "Our cities are besieged. Our suburban areas have become infected. Even our rural areas are now feeling the shock effect."

Pepper's assessment of the situation was somewhat exaggerated, but it was true that drug use was on the rise. As demand for drugs grew, suppliers rushed to fill that demand. Drug traffickers smuggled heroin into the United States from Southwest Asia and cocaine from Latin America. Marijuana came from Mexico, as well as from growers in the United States.

A LINE IN THE SAND

In 1971 President Richard Nixon declared that drug abuse was "public enemy number one" in the United States. He coined the phrase War on Drugs and set out to win that war. To that end, the Nixon administration increased funding for drug treatment and enforcement, passed stronger antidrug laws, and created the Drug Enforcement Administration (DEA) to oversee government antidrug programs.

The new War on Drugs was not going to be easy. Traffickers could make millions of dollars selling drugs in the United States. In the South American nation of Colombia, cocaine traffickers organized themselves into cartels, or business alliances, to more efficiently supply cocaine to customers in the United States. With massive drug profits, they were able to employ airplanes, boats, and other vehicles to keep the drugs moving. The cartels did not hesitate to use murder, kidnapping, and other violence to protect their businesses. They fought law enforcement and rival drug traffickers with high-powered weapons.

Back in the United States, drug use became increasingly woven into the fabric of everyday life. Many young people routinely smoked marijuana. Cocaine use became fashionable among some upper-class white Americans.

Meanwhile, the U.S. government worked harder than ever to fight the drug traffickers. In addition to the DEA, the U.S. Customs Service, the Federal Bureau of Investigation (FBI), the Internal Revenue Service, and the U.S. Coast Guard joined the fight. The U.S. government allocated more and more money for the War on Drugs. These efforts produced some impressive successes. Drug agents regularly interdicted (stopped and seized) massive shipments of cocaine and other drugs at the U.S. border. But more drugs kept pouring across.

JUST SAY NO

Americans held many different opinions on the nation's drug problem. Some people thought that increased law enforcement was the answer. Others thought

Above: Federal agents confiscate a truck full of cocaine at the U.S.–Mexican border in the late 1970s.

that more funding for drug education and treatment made sense. They figured that reducing the demand for drugs in the United States—by helping people stop using drugs or convincing them not to start in the first place—would help put the drug traffickers out of business. In 1984 Nancy Reagan, the wife of President Ronald Reagan, added her voice to the drug debate. She encouraged young people to "Just Say No" to drug use.

That slogan became the centerpiece of her husband's antidrug campaign.

Drug use took its worst toll in inner-city neighborhoods. There, many people struggled with poverty and unemployment. For some inner-city residents, the mind-altering effects of drug use offered a temporary escape from hopelessness and despair. For others, dealing drugs provided a good source of income in places where steady jobs were hard to find. But both drug use and drug dealing hurt the surrounding community. Many drug users committed burglaries to get the cash needed to support their drug habits. Drug dealers fought and sometimes killed one another to protect their turf. Sometimes they accidentally killed innocent bystanders.

Crack cocaine appeared in New York City and other urban centers in 1985. This smokable form of cocaine was cheap and highly addictive. Crack use made the problems of poor inner-city neighborhoods even worse. The Reagan administration sounded the alarm about crack cocaine. Newspapers reported on "crack babies." These children of crack-using mothers had been exposed to cocaine in the womb and were born with a physical addiction to the drug.

In October 1986, President Reagan signed a tough law

Above: President Ronald Reagan and his wife, Nancy, were at the forefront of the War on Drugs in the 1980s.

> ## " The day of tolerance for those who break the law in using drugs is over. "
>
> —PRESIDENT GEORGE H. W. BUSH
> **☀ USA TODAY** · AUGUST 16, 1989

called the Anti-Drug Abuse Act. This legislation increased funding for the War on Drugs. It also created mandatory minimum sentences for drug users and drug dealers. For instance, anyone convicted of selling 5 grams (0.2 ounces) or more of crack cocaine automatically received a five-year prison sentence. Judges were not allowed to hand out lighter sentences, no matter what the circumstances. Under the new law, more and more Americans ended up in prison on drug offenses.

Not only the federal government but also states, employers, schools, and other organizations took strong stands against drug use in this era. New York, Michigan, and other states passed extremely tough laws, with long prison sentences for selling or owning small amounts of illegal drugs. Meanwhile, some companies created drug-testing programs for employees and job applicants. People who tested positive for drug use could be fired or weren't hired to begin with. Schools also instituted drug testing. They punished students who tested positive for drugs with suspension, ejection from sports teams, and other penalties.

KINDER AND GENTLER

Most Americans of the late twentieth century realized that punishment and prison could go only so far in ridding the nation of illegal drugs. Many people preferred a more compassionate approach. They recognized that drug addiction is a medical and psychological issue as well as a law enforcement issue. They also saw that drug use and abuse were tightly bound up with other social ills—everything from stress to poverty to child abuse.

Throughout the late twentieth century, educators, doctors, and mental health professionals studied drug use and drug addiction. They wanted to find the best ways to treat drug addicts and to keep people off drugs in the first place. Government and private organizations set up many drug education and drug treatment programs.

A new approach to dealing with drug offenders emerged in the 1990s. This was the drug court program, which sends nonviolent drug offenders to mandatory drug treatment programs instead of prison. The program began in Dade County, Florida, and quickly spread to other communities. Many people who went through drug-court treatment were able to stay off drugs afterward.

Meanwhile, the debate over drug use grew more complicated when studies began to show that marijuana was

Below: Health workers use a variety of treatments to help addicts overcome drug addiction. At this program in Baltimore, Maryland, a man receives an acupuncture treatment.

effective in treating certain health problems, such as pain and severe nausea. Some doctors said they would prescribe marijuana to cancer, AIDS, and other patients if it were legal to do so. Several states established medical marijuana programs to legally provide marijuana to certain patients. The federal government denounced these efforts and shut down some of them. Drug enforcement officials pointed to additional studies that showed the harm of marijuana use, such as lung damage and short-term memory loss.

A NEW CENTURY

The arrival of the twenty-first century marked thirty years of the U.S. War on Drugs. After thirty years, was the war working? The answers were mixed. According to the DEA, cocaine use had dropped by 70 percent between 1988 and 2003, and heroin use had dropped by 33 percent in roughly the same period. At the same time, however, the use of other drugs had risen. One government-funded study reported that between 1991 and 2002, marijuana use had risen among U.S. youths—with a 30 percent increase for twelfth graders, a 65 percent increase for tenth graders, and an 88 percent increase for eighth graders. What's more, new drugs, including Ecstasy and methamphetamines, had arrived in U.S. communities in the 1990s. Americans were using the new

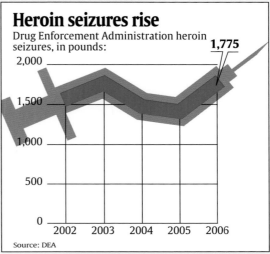

USA TODAY Snapshots®

Heroin seizures rise

Drug Enforcement Administration heroin seizures, in pounds:

1,775

Source: DEA

By David Stuckey and Sam Ward, USA TODAY, 2007

drugs in increasing numbers. Some Americans also abused prescription drugs, such as the painkiller OxyContin. People bought and sold such drugs illegally and used them without a doctor's oversight.

In the face of mixed results, antidrug forces fought on. In the first decade of the 2000s, the federal government spent about $20 billion per year on drug control, including law enforcement, treatment, and education. Law officers arrested about 1.9 million Americans each year for drug offenses. Government agents seized and destroyed tons of illegal drugs.

U.S. government agents also took the fight against drugs right to the source—all the way to South American coca growers in Colombia, Peru, and Bolivia. U.S. agents sprayed coca crops with chemicals to kill the plants. They encouraged South American farmers to switch to growing legal crops, such as bananas, corn, citrus fruits, and coffee. These programs had only limited success. Some South American growers did switch to legal crops. But coca growing

Above: Soldiers destroy coca plants on a plantation in Colombia. The United States works with South American governments to wipe out drug crops.

> ## "A balanced approach of prevention, enforcement, and treatment is the key in the fight against drugs.
>
> **—DRUG ENFORCEMENT ADMINISTRATION,** 2003

earned them up to ten times more, so they quickly returned to coca.

And as U.S. agents cracked down on drug operations in South America, trafficking increased in Mexico, just south of the United States. Backed by vast amounts of cash and high-powered weaponry, Mexican drug cartels smuggled tons of cocaine, marijuana, heroin, and methamphetamines over the U.S. border to distribution networks in the United States. They bribed government officials and frequently murdered officials who tried to stop them. Even the efforts of the Mexican military could not slow the cartels. Violence raged in Mexican border towns as the drug gangs battled law enforcement and battled one another over territory.

Above: Mexican army troops hunt for drug traffickers along the border after a shootout in 2009.

Mexican cartels plague Atlanta

From the Pages of
USA TODAY In a city where Coca Cola, United Parcel Service and Home Depot are the titans of industry, there are new powerful forces on the block: Mexican drug cartels.

Their presence and ruthless tactics are largely unknown to most here. Yet, of the 195 U.S. cities where Mexican drug-trafficking organizations are operating, federal law enforcement officials say Atlanta has emerged as the new gateway to the troubled Southwest border.

Rival drug cartels, the same violent groups warring in Mexico for control of routes to lucrative U.S. markets, have established Atlanta as the principal distribution center for the entire eastern U.S., according to the Justice Department's National Drug Intelligence Center.

In fiscal year 2008, federal drug authorities seized more drug-related cash in Atlanta—about $70 million—than any other region in the country, Drug Enforcement Administration (DEA) records show.

This year, more than $30 million has been intercepted in the Atlanta area—far more than the $19 million in Los Angeles and $18 million in Chicago.

Atlanta has not seen a fraction of the violence that engulfs much of northern Mexico, but law enforcement officials are increasingly concerned about the cartels' expanding operations here.

"The same folks who are rolling heads in the streets of Ciudad Juarez"—El Paso's Mexican neighbor—"are operating in Atlanta. Here, they are just better behaved," says Jack Killorin, who heads the Office of National Drug Control Policy's federal task force in Atlanta.

The same regional features that appeal to legitimate corporate operations—access to transportation systems and proximity to major U.S. cities—have lured the cartels, Atlanta U.S. Attorney David Nahmias says.

From the border, shipments of marijuana, cocaine, methamphetamine and heroin are routed over land to Atlanta for storage in a network of stash houses. They are then moved to distribution operations in the Carolinas, Tennessee, the Mid-Atlantic, New York and New England.

Cash is generally moved over the same routes back to the Atlanta area, where balance sheets are reconciled. The bundles of money are turned over to transportation units for bulk shipments back to Mexico, [Atlanta DEA chief Rodney] Benson says.

Although the level of drug-related violence in Mexico has not surfaced in the Atlanta area, recent incidents have raised concerns among law enforcement officials.

Last July, for example, a Rhode Island man who allegedly owed $300,000 to Atlanta-based traffickers was found chained to a wall in the basement of a Lilburn, Ga., home, located in western Gwinnett County.

Benson says the man had been blindfolded, gagged and beaten. Federal investigators, who were alerted to the location, later found the man alive but severely dehydrated. Three Mexican nationals fled the house when authorities approached. All three were captured and a cache of weapons, including an assault rifle, was seized. "There is no doubt in my mind that . . . we certainly saved his life," Benson says.

About the same time last year, another man was kidnapped in Gwinnett County for non-payment of drug proceeds. When traffickers went to pick up what they thought was a $2 million ransom, shots were exchanged between the traffickers and police who were working with the victim's family. One of the suspects was killed and the other arrested, Benson says.

Killorin says much of the violence has been related to similar incidents of "intra-cartel discipline" and has not spilled into the streets.

There is no mistaking the groups' influence.

"We know they're here," Gwinnett County Police Cpl. Illana Spellman says, adding that the area's access to interstate highways is a major lure. "Geographically, it's set up perfectly for these kinds of activities."

—Larry Copeland and Kevin Johnson

Above: Mexican soldiers seize marijuana during a drug bust along the Mexican–U.S. border in 2009.

Meanwhile, the violence in Mexico began to spill across the border to U.S. cities such as Tucson, Arizona, and San Diego, California. Some Mexican drug cartels also began to grow marijuana on remote and poorly policed public lands in the United States, a tactic that was safer and easier than smuggling it across the border from Mexico. Americans became worried. The United States seemed no closer to winning the War on Drugs, and that war was coming closer to home.

FRESH FACES AT THE TOP

The election of Barack Obama as president of the United States in 2008 put a new Democratic administration in the White House. Obama appointed Gil Kerlikowske, formerly the police chief of Seattle, as head of the Office of National Drug Control Policy—a position informally known as the drug czar. The new president faced a host of problems when he took office, and the drug trade was certainly one of them. How would Obama and his new government tackle the problem? Joe Biden, Obama's vice president, vowed "to bring the [drug] situation under control, to protect our people, and to bring about the demise of the Mexican drug cartels."

The vice president sounded determined and confident, but would the same old War on Drugs be enough? And if the War on Drugs was such a good strategy, why did the nation's drug problem appear to be getting worse? Faced with these questions, some Americans took a radical stance. They said that, in fact, the War on Drugs wasn't working. They even argued that the War on Drugs was making the drug problem worse. What did they propose instead? To many, their idea sounded extreme—even outrageous. The answer to the nation's drug problem, some argued, was not to amplify the War on Drugs but instead to stop that war altogether. The answer, they argued, was to legalize drugs.

CHAPTER THREE

A Lost Cause?

THOSE WHO ARGUE FOR DRUG LEGALIZATION MAKE A two-part argument. First, they say, the U.S. War on Drugs is not working—that it is doing more harm than good. Second, they argue, the way to solve the U.S. drug problem is not to fight and punish drug sellers and users but instead to make their activities *legal*. To understand the second argument, we must examine the first.

At first glance, the War on Drugs makes a lot of sense. Drugs are harmful substances that can destroy lives and even whole communities. The United States has allocated great amounts of money and person-power to keeping drugs out of the nation and to punishing those who sell and use them. What's wrong with that?

Legalization forces say that a lot is wrong with the War on Drugs. Let's look at their arguments.

Left: Many people disagree with U.S. drug policy and attend protest rallies to voice their views. The majority of these protesters want marijuana to be legalized for medicinal use.

A NO-WIN SITUATION?

Every year, the United States spends more and more money on the War on Drugs. When the war began, in 1972, the government allocated $65 million to fund the DEA. Thirty-three years later, in 2005, DEA yearly funding was $2.1 billion. That's more than a thirty-two-fold increase. And that's just for the DEA. When you add in the budgets of other federal drug-control agencies and programs, the dollar amount rises to almost $20 billion a year. Add in state and local drug budgets, and the total is more like $44 billion per year. Ultimately, it is U.S. citizens who foot the bill for the war via their tax dollars. What do Americans get for all that money?

Does $44 billion a year buy us drug-free schools and drug-free inner cities? Does $44 billion a year shut down drug cartels? Does $44 billion a year

Above: DEA agents seize millions of dollars worth of drugs each year, but their seizures are barely making a dent in the drug market.

keep rival drug gangs from killing one another, killing police officers, and sometimes killing innocent bystanders? Does $44 billion a year prevent the sorrow and suffering caused by drug addiction?

Critics of the War on Drugs say that the massive U.S. drug budget hasn't fixed any of these problems. Despite bigger and bigger budgets, the drug problem has only increased in the United States. "There's been more harm done by the drug war than good," says Norm Stamper, a retired police chief and Drug War opponent. "We have spent a trillion dollars prosecuting that war since Richard Nixon proclaimed drugs public enemy number one and declared all-out war against them. And what do we have to show for it? While rates can fluctuate, drugs are more readily available today at lower prices and higher levels of potency than ever before."

Certainly, the War on Drugs has not kept drugs out of the

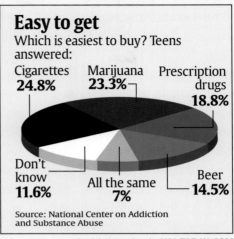

Easy to get

Which is easiest to buy? Teens answered:

Cigarettes **24.8%** Marijuana **23.3%** Prescription drugs **18.8%**

Don't know **11.6%** All the same **7%** Beer **14.5%**

Source: National Center on Addiction and Substance Abuse

By Adrienne Lewis, USA TODAY, 2008

hands of teenagers. Nic Sheff, who started smoking marijuana at the age of twelve and later became addicted to methamphetamines, told his father that in his neighborhood in Marin County, California, marijuana was easier for teenagers to get than alcohol. Surveys show that almost 60 percent of high school seniors have tried an illegal drug at least once. Almost 33 percent of seniors currently use drugs.

BEHIND BARS

Every year, authorities arrest about 1.9 million Americans for drug law violations. That's more people than the entire population of New Mexico. The arrestees range from teenage marijuana smokers to large-scale drug traffickers. In 2009 more than five hundred thousand Americans were in prison for drug offenses. That's more than a tenfold increase since 1980, when the number of drug offenders in prison was just forty-one thousand.

Have all the arrests and prison sentences helped rid the nation of illegal drugs? Once again, Drug War opponents say no. Illegal drugs are more widely available than ever, even with five hundred thousand drug offenders in jail.

By arresting and imprisoning drug users, "you are getting people, not drugs, off the streets," explains Dorothy Gaines, who was imprisoned for a drug offense in the 1990s and has since become an anti–Drug War activist. Jack A. Cole, executive director of Law Enforcement Against Prohibition (LEAP), echoes that argument. He writes, "This is not a war on drugs—it's a war on people."

Having worked in law enforcement for more than twenty-five years—mostly as an undercover narcotics officer—Cole has seen drug use and the Drug War up close. And he believes that being arrested for drug use is actually far more harmful than drug use itself. Cole explains that most people arrested for drug offenses pay a steep price. In addition to jail time, the court might take away their driver's licenses for six months. If they are college students, the government might cut off their student loans. And if a drug offender lives in public

> " **There are a lot of Derrick Currys in [prison]. They are not monsters. They are kids who made mistakes.**"
>
> —ARTHUR CURRY, WHOSE SON DERRICK WAS SENTENCED TO NINETEEN YEARS IN PRISON FOR A CRACK OFFENSE
>
> USA TODAY · DECEMBER 22, 2000

Above: Inmates watch television inside a prison. Drug War opponents say that locking up drug offenders is the wrong solution to the U.S. drug problem.

housing, the housing authority can evict not only the offender but also his or her family members—whether or not they had any role in the drug offense.

Even after an offender serves jail time and other punishments expire, he or she will never be completely free of the drug conviction. The arrest will remain on his or her permanent record. Employers often refuse to hire people who have been arrested for drug offenses.

Everyone agrees that people who break the law should be punished. But does it make sense to arrest a teenager or young adult who experiments briefly with marijuana or cocaine?

A War on Minorities

Opponents often charge that the War on Drugs is a racist one. They note that law enforcement focuses most of its drug-control efforts on inner-city neighborhoods and the minority groups that live there. According to law and philosophy professor Douglas Husak, percentages of drug users are roughly the same for whites and African Americans. Yet African Americans make up more than 62 percent of drug offenders in state prisons. In Illinois a black man is fifty-seven times more likely than a white man to go to prison on drug charges.

Drug War critics charge that corrupt police officers sometimes use the drug laws to single out minorities for punishment. A case in Tulia, Texas, is the most infamous example. In July 1999, police in Tulia arrested forty-three residents on drug charges. Forty of the arrestees were African Americans. Tulia's sheriff had orchestrated the arrests with the assistance of an undercover officer named Tom Coleman. Coleman claimed to have bought

Above: Thirteen defendants in the Tulia, Texas, drug case sit on trial in a Swisher County, Texas, courtroom in 2003.

> ## " In New York, 93% of the people in jail under the draconian drug laws are African-American and Latino, even though there are likely a number of white people on Wall Street who use cocaine. "

—**TONY NEWMAN,** DRUG POLICY ALLIANCE

USA TODAY · OCTOBER 19, 2005

cocaine and other drugs from the arrestees. But he presented no tape recordings, photographs, notes, eyewitnesses, or other evidence to back up his claims. Police found no money, drugs, or weapons in the homes of the suspected drug dealers. No matter. The cases proceeded through court. Some of the arrestees were convicted and sentenced to long prison terms—one for ninety-nine years. Meanwhile, the racist aspects of the case were apparent. The arresting officers and the juries that convicted the suspects were all white. Coleman and other officers routinely used racial epithets in describing the drug suspects. Coleman and the white residents of Tulia seemed to be mainly interested in locking up African Americans, using drug offenses as an excuse.

When the national media and civil rights groups took a closer look, it became clear that Tom Coleman, not the drug suspects, was the real criminal. He was wanted for theft in another town. After going to work for the sheriff in Tulia, he claimed to have made one hundred drug purchases there, yet some of the suspected "drug dealers" were not even in town on the days they had allegedly sold drugs to Coleman. Gradually, the suspects began to clear their names, but not before many of them served several years in prison.

Consider that presidents Bill Clinton and Barack Obama both admitted to experimenting with illegal drugs as young men. Under U.S. drug laws, they should have been arrested and punished. They should have had to deal with the legal consequences of their actions. But they didn't. Neither man was caught using drugs or was punished for it. With clean police records, both men pursued careers in politics and ended up in the nation's highest office.

Would society have benefited if Barack Obama had been put in jail for his youthful cocaine use? Drug War opponents say no. They say that those who briefly experiment with drugs are not hurting anyone—that they should be free to pursue their lives and careers without punishment and a police record dogging them forever afterward.

Opponents further point to privacy issues. After all, what people do in their own

Below: Both former president Bill Clinton *(left)* and President Barack Obama admitted to experimenting with drugs as young men. It's not uncommon for young people to try drugs briefly and then move on.

Above: A sheriff's deputy arrests a young man for growing marijuana in his home.

homes and to their own bodies shouldn't be anyone else's business, should it? "There has to be something wrong with a law that says that what you do in the privacy of your own home, by yourself or with friends or loved ones—that the cops have the right to arrest you irrespective of whatever harm you've done to anybody else," argues Ethan Nadelmann, head of the Drug Policy Alliance, the nation's leading pro-legalization group.

Opponents of the Drug War say the government simply goes too far, aggressively pursuing drug users who may or may not be hurting anyone.

MODERN-DAY PROHIBITION

Laws are supposed to keep people safe. They are supposed to keep society running in an orderly fashion. They are supposed to be applied fairly and justly. Most laws work as intended. But sometimes, laws backfire.

Obama's folly of youth shouldn't hinder rise

From the Pages of USA TODAY

I knew it would come to this. The widespread adulation that Barack Obama received with the release last year of his second book, *The Audacity of Hope*, pushed the junior U.S. senator from Illinois to begin making soundings about a run for the presidency in 2008. And the initial response was downright giddy.

During visits to Iowa and New Hampshire—early testing grounds for presidential hopefuls—women swooned over Obama, and men rushed to be photographed with the man NBC News' Meredith Vieira called a political "rock star." Seasoned journalists gushingly spoke of Obama as a new force in U.S. politics who has chased everyone except New York Sen. Hillary Clinton from the field of viable contenders for the Democratic Party's 2008 presidential nomination.

But Obama's meteoric rise felt the pull of a political black hole last week when The *Washington Post* reported that in an earlier book, he had admitted to using illegal drugs while in high school and college.

"Junkie. Pothead. That's where I'd been headed: the final, fatal role of the young would-be black man. Except the highs hadn't been about that, me trying to prove what a down brother I was.... I got high for just the opposite effect, something that could push questions of who I

Above: Barack Obama greets fans at a book signing in 2006.

was out of my mind, something that could flatten out the landscape of my heart, blur the edges of my memory," Obama wrote about the reasons for his youthful experimentation with marijuana and cocaine.

Far from being a prelude to his flirtation with presidential politics, this admission came before Obama entered political life. It was a catharsis—the kind of revelation about a troubled time that can produce emotional freedom and moral rejuvenation.

But in the world of politics, such honesty often runs afoul of the holier-than-thou crowd. I suspect, it's why Bill Clinton, when confronted on the issue, admitted having smoked marijuana but tried to mitigate this offense by saying he never inhaled. And I think it explains why George W. Bush deflected questions about his suspected drug use by quipping: "When I was young and irresponsible, I was young and irresponsible."

Like many other young people of his generation, Obama experimented with illegal drugs. That's nothing to be proud of—and what he wrote in his first book, *Dreams from My Father*, doesn't come across that way. But it is a window into the thinking of a young man who, like his country, struggles with the issue of race and identity.

"Everybody was welcome into the club of disaffection," Obama wrote of that period in his life. "And if the high didn't solve whatever it was that was getting you down, it could at least help you laugh at the world's ongoing folly and see through all the hypocrisy . . . and cheap moralism."

Fortunately for Obama, he escaped that reckless period with no apparent, lasting damage. And fortunately for the rest of us, many Americans are willing to excuse such bad behavior by public officials when it happened in the distant past—and the person in question has moved on to a better life.

I don't know if Obama is of presidential timber. I don't know if he possesses the deep intellect, courage and character that this nation so badly needs in its chief executive. I don't know if he is as studious as he is bright; or if he is as feeling as he is outspoken about the problems of this nation's old and poor.

But what I do know is this: Given the candor and honesty with which he revealed his youthful drug use, and the fact that he did so long before mounting the national political stage, Barack Obama deserves to be judged on his public service, not some old demons.

He deserves to be given a chance to show us the kind of man he has become—and the kind of president he could be.

—DeWayne Wickham, from the Opinion page

One of the most striking examples is the Prohibition law, which banned the manufacture, sale, and transport of alcoholic beverages in the United States.

Most people agree that Prohibition was a failure. The law was intended to ban drinking in the United States, yet Americans continued to drink. And because they couldn't buy booze via legal distribution networks, they turned to the black market. The liquor that people purchased from speakeasies and other illegal sellers was high priced and sometimes poisonous. Prohibition agents were unable to shut down all the illegal manufacturers and sellers. Some agents even got into the illegal liquor business themselves. The big winners during Prohibition were the gangsters and bootleggers who made hefty profits supplying

Above: Speakeasies flourished during Prohibition. Thousands popped up in urban areas.

Above: Antonio Maria Costa *(left)*, executive director of the United Nations Office on Drugs and Crime, speaks about drugs and corruption at a 2008 conference.

the booze. The losers were U.S. citizens, who saw crime and corruption increase during the Prohibition years.

Critics of the War on Drugs say the similarities to modern times are striking. They say that modern-day drug prohibition has led to lawlessness and disorder, much the way Prohibition did in the 1920s. In the 1920s, bootleggers fought one another to protect their turf. They hijacked one another's liquor trucks. They raided one another's warehouses. Since their business

was illegal, they couldn't use the courts to resolve their disputes—so they took the law into their own hands. In Chicago alone, almost eight hundred gangsters died in shootouts with other gangsters during the thirteen years of Prohibition. This kind of violence and lawlessness was unheard of in the years before Prohibition.

Opponents say that drug prohibition has created the same situation in modern times. Like the 1920s gangsters, modern-day drug suppliers carry out drive-by shootings, cartel kidnappings, and other violent acts because they can't resolve their disagreements legally. Rather than keeping society safe and orderly, opponents say, the drug laws have created a violent business underworld in which disorder reigns.

Many people point to another parallel with Prohibition. During that era, corruption was rife. Many police officers, politicians, and Prohibition Bureau agents took bribes from bootleggers, who were rolling in cash because their business was so profitable. In the most typical scenario, a bootlegger paid law officers and other officials to "look the other way" and not interfere with bootlegging operations. In extreme cases, some government agents worked hand-in-hand with the bootleggers, partnering with them in sales of illegal liquor. Some Prohibition agents even sold the illegal liquor they had confiscated.

In the modern Drug War, those scenarios have been updated to the twenty-first century. In a number of cases, police officers have been charged with taking bribes from drug dealers, transporting drugs for dealers, and selling drugs themselves. Like the bootleggers before them, the drug dealers are flush with cash. Paying off cops can be an easy way to get the law off their backs. Most police officers are honest, but some give in to temptation. "Exposed to suitcase after suitcase of illegal cash and drugs," writes the Drug Policy Alliance, "many officers can't resist helping themselves."

In Latin America, corruption has reached into the highest levels of government. With their vast drug profits, groups such as the Medellin cartel in Colombia have been able to bribe politicians and law enforcement officials. In some Mexican towns, drug cartels allegedly have the entire police force on the payroll.

Critics say that the modern War on Drugs has created an additional kind of corruption. Often, politicians and the public put pressure on police departments to win the War on Drugs.

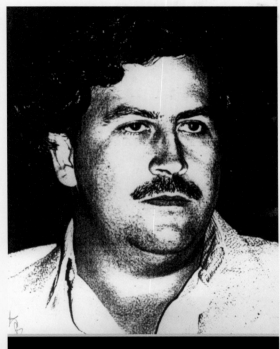

Above: Pablo Escobar was head of the powerful Medellin drug cartel in Colombia. A special police unit tracked him down and shot him in 1993.

For continued government funding, the police must show results—a record of winning convictions and locking up drug dealers. Some officers try to win these convictions at any cost—even at the expense of truth and justice. In numerous cases, U.S. police officers have been found guilty of lying on the witness stand, conducting illegal searches, planting drugs on suspects, and tampering with evidence to win convictions. Opponents say these crimes are an ugly extension of the War on Drugs. If the government wasn't so eager to catch and punish drug offenders, critics say, police corruption would decline.

PUSH-DOWN, POP-UP

Can the War on Drugs ever be won? Can we stop the flow of illegal drugs into and within the United States? Law enforcement agents have tried to do so tirelessly. They've arrested drug dealers, shut down methamphetamine labs, sprayed poisonous chemicals on coca crops in South America, and battled with drug cartels.

Black and White: Crack versus Powdered Cocaine

Nowhere is the racial disparity in the Drug War more apparent than in federal sentencing guidelines for powdered and crack cocaine. The two drugs are very similar. Crack gives users a fast, intense high when they smoke it. Powdered cocaine gives a similar high when mixed with water and injected and a slower, less intense high when snorted.

In the mid-1980s, newspapers printed alarming stories about the scourge of crack in inner-city neighborhoods. In the wake of media attention, Congress passed harsh mandatory minimum sentencing laws for crack cocaine. Under the new laws, a person convicted of possessing 5 grams (0.2 ounces) of crack with intent to distribute it faced a minimum of five years in prison. Contrast

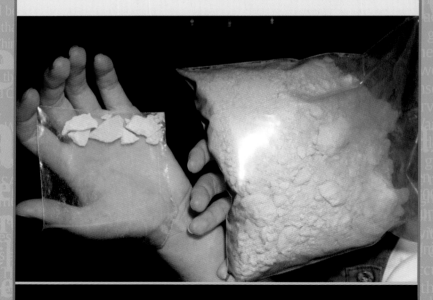

A DEA agent holds 5 grams (0.2 ounces) of crack cocaine *(left)* and 500 grams (18 ounces) of cocaine powder. Selling either bag will get the seller at least five years in jail.

this with the sentencing rules for powdered cocaine, which impose the same five-year prison sentence for possession of 500 grams (18 ounces) with intent to distribute. Thus the law is one hundred times more severe for crack cocaine than for powdered cocaine. Lawmakers who passed the harsh crack laws in the 1980s did so under the impression that crack is much more addictive than powdered cocaine and causes users to behave violently—notions that have since been disproven.

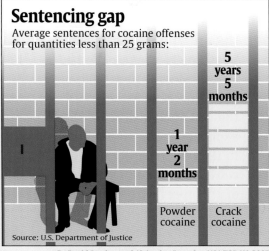

USA TODAY Snapshots®

Sentencing gap
Average sentences for cocaine offenses for quantities less than 25 grams:

5 years 5 months

1 year 2 months

Powder cocaine

Crack cocaine

Source: U.S. Department of Justice

By David Stuckey and Alejandro Gonzalez, USA TODAY, 2007

Critics have long pointed out that powdered cocaine users tend to be white, while crack cocaine users are more likely to be black. Thus the law indirectly discriminates against black drug offenders by subjecting them to much harsher standards than their white counterparts.

Over the years, many groups have pressured Congress to change the crack sentencing guidelines to bring them more in line with guidelines for cocaine and other drugs—without success. The Obama administration has indicated that it does plan to change the law, however.

In every case, the authorities have come up against the "push-down, pop-up" effect. That is, when you push down the drug trade in one area, it pops up elsewhere. "We had a lot of success a few years ago in taking down a number of the Colombian drug dealers," explained President Bill Clinton in 1999, "but one of the adverse consequences of that was a lot of the operations were moved north to Mexico."

Similarly, when the police arrest a drug dealer or destroy a meth lab in the United States, other dealers quickly rush in to take over the business. "When I arrested a drug dealer the number of drug sales didn't change at all," Jack Cole recalls about his days on the narcotics squad. "I was simply creating a job opening for a long line of people more than willing to risk arrest for those obscene profits."

Cole says that the push-down, pop-up effect works with individual drugs too. In the early years of his career, in the 1970s, police had success in thwarting marijuana smugglers. Marijuana is bulky and easy to smell inside a truck or other vehicle. But Cole explains that "the successful interdiction of large amounts of marijuana . . . caused many marijuana dealers to switch to harder drugs that were less detectable and far more profitable, pound for pound."

As long as there's a demand

USA TODAY Snapshots®

Illegal cargo

Pounds of cocaine seized by Coast Guard by fiscal year:

Year	Pounds
2003	136,865
2004	242,435
2005	303,662
2006	234,337
2007	238,040

Source: U.S. Coast Guard

By David Stuckey and Veronica Salazar, USA TODAY, 2008

> ❝ **I feel very strongly we [Americans] have a co-responsibility. Our insatiable demand for illegal drugs fuels the drug trade.** ❞
>
> **—U.S. SECRETARY OF STATE HILLARY CLINTON,**
> DISCUSSING MEXICAN DRUG CARTELS
>
> **USA TODAY · MARCH 26, 2009**

for drugs, suppliers will emerge to fill that demand, observe Drug War opponents. They say the public's insatiable demand for drugs and the eager and vast army of suppliers makes the War on Drugs ultimately unwinnable. The Drug Policy Alliance sums the situation up this way: "Day in and day out police officers see one arrested drug seller replaced by another. No matter how much illegal drugs are seized and confiscated, more pours in." So is the War on Drugs a lost cause? As we'll learn in the next chapter, many people are quick to say no.

CHAPTER FOUR

A War Worth Fighting

DRUG WAR OPPONENTS SAY THE WAR ON DRUGS IS unwinnable—and therefore, it should be abandoned. But to Americans who support the Drug War, this argument is defeatist. Just because a war is difficult and includes setbacks as well as victories, that doesn't mean we shouldn't fight it, they say.

In March 2008, the George W. Bush administration presented its *National Drug Control Strategy 2008 Annual Report*. This document outlines three goals of U.S. drug policy: "Stopping Drug Use before It Starts" (through education), "Healing America's Drug Users" (through drug treatment programs), and "Disrupting the Market for Illegal Drugs" (through law-enforcement efforts).

According to the report, the United States has made impressive progress in the War on Drugs. The report states that between 2001 and 2008, marijuana use

Left: John Walters speaks at a press conference about U.S. drug policy. Walters was drug czar during the George W. Bush administration.

among teenagers fell by 24 percent, teen Ecstasy use dropped by more than 50 percent, and overall youth drug use dropped by 24 percent. The report goes on to chronicle a variety of government antidrug programs, including drug testing in schools and workplaces, drug abuse education, antidrug media campaigns, drug treatment programs, and law-enforcement efforts within the United States, along the U.S. border, and in foreign countries.

Drug War supporters acknowledge that it's probably impossible to stop *all* drug use in the United States. But that's not the goal says Barry McCaffrey, drug czar under former president Bill Clinton. McCaffrey explains that the government's goal is to *reduce* drug use in the United States, and in that sense, the government *is* winning the War on Drugs. Those who back the Drug War point to countless victories—not just in arresting and punishing drug traffickers

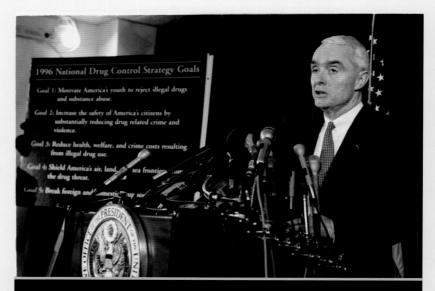

Above: Barry McCaffrey holds a press conference during his time as drug czar in the late 1990s.

USA TODAY Snapshots®

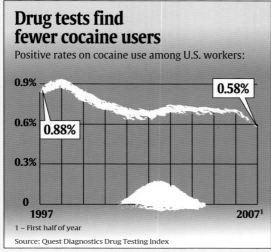

Drug tests find fewer cocaine users

Positive rates on cocaine use among U.S. workers:

0.88%

0.58%

1997   2007[1]

1 – First half of year

Source: Quest Diagnostics Drug Testing Index

By Jae Yang and Veronica Salazar, USA TODAY, 2007

but also in treating drug addicts, educating Americans about drug abuse, and keeping people off drugs in the first place.

LAW AS PREVENTION

Opponents of the Drug War say that people who are determined to get drugs will always find a way to get them. Opponents say that laws haven't stopped people from buying drugs. After all, every year, Americans purchase $60 billion worth of illegal drugs. Clearly, the fact that drug use is against the law hasn't stopped them.

But Drug War defenders disagree with this argument. They say that drug laws do provide a barrier to drug use. Consider the experience of Charles Van Deventer, an advertising copywriter from Manhattan. In 2001 Van Deventer wrote an opinion piece for *Newsweek* magazine titled "I'm Proof: The War on Drugs Is Working." In this piece, Van Deventer described how he and friends used drugs casually for a while. He felt he was growing close to addiction. But buying illegal drugs wasn't easy. Van Deventer and his friends feared being arrested. They worried about undercover cops posing as drug dealers. And they didn't like doing business with real drug dealers, who often sold them fake drugs.

Van Deventer didn't want to be a lawbreaker, and he believes that saved him from the point of no return—the point where casual drug use turned into addiction. "The more barriers there are—be they the cops or the hassle or the fear of dying [from an overdose]—the less likely you are to get addicted," he wrote. He concluded, "The road to addiction was just bumpy enough that I chose not to go down it. In this sense, we are winning the war on drugs just by fighting them."

While it's certainly true that some people will jump through endless hoops to get drugs, no matter what the cost or legal consequences, Charles Van Deventer wasn't one of them.

Drug War proponents say that his experiences mirror those of many other young Americans. They say that drug laws are a form of prevention—one of several barriers to the tragedy of addiction—and that it's crucial that these laws be tough and vigorously enforced.

CRIME AND VIOLENCE

Drug War opponents often say that drug use is a "victimless crime." They admit that some addicts steal to get money to buy drugs, but they argue that drug use *on its own* does not usually cause violence or criminal behavior. They stress that most people who use drugs do so in private, without breaking other laws or bothering other people. It's true that a user might damage his or her own health with drug use, but it makes no sense, Drug War opponents argue, to punish people who are not hurting anyone else.

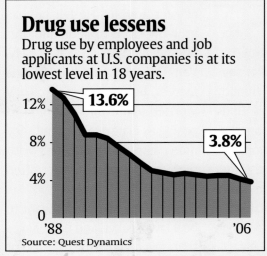

Drug use lessens

Drug use by employees and job applicants at U.S. companies is at its lowest level in 18 years.

13.6%

3.8%

'88   '06

Source: Quest Dynamics

By Julie Snider, USA TODAY, 2007

What about Prescription Drugs?

Certain drugs are legal to take with a doctor's prescription. If your doctor prescribes OxyContin, Xanax, or another drug for pain or anxiety, it's perfectly legal for you to take it. But if you sell the drugs to someone else or take them without a prescription, you're breaking the law.

In recent decades, the illegal selling of prescription drugs has become big business. And more and more Americans are becoming addicted to prescription drugs. OxyContin is especially addictive and dangerous. When taken in combination with alcohol or other drugs, it can be deadly.

When doctors prescribe drugs such as OxyContin, they closely monitor the doses to make sure that patients don't become addicted. This system usually works, although some people still become hooked, even under a doctor's care. When people take prescription drugs without a doctor's supervision, their chances of becoming addicted are much greater.

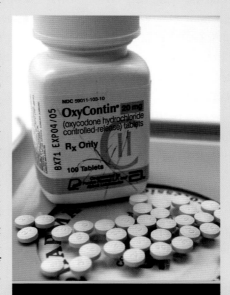

Above: Prescription drugs such as OxyContin are especially dangerous when taken without a doctor's supervision.

> ## "This generation is abusing far fewer illegal drugs than any generation before them, but prescription drugs are a problem."
>
> —**STEVE PASIERB,** PARTNERSHIP FOR A DRUG-FREE AMERICA
> **USA TODAY · SEPTEMBER 5, 2008**

Drug War supporters strongly disagree with this argument. They say that drug users frequently hurt a lot of people besides themselves. A DEA publication explains that "drug use changes behavior and exacerbates criminal activity. . . . Drugs often cause people to do things they wouldn't do if they were rational and free of the influence of drugs."

The DEA cites several statistics to support this claim. One study found that half of all people arrested for violent crimes test positive for drugs at the time of their arrest. Another study revealed that 24 percent of people who attack police officers are under the influence of drugs at the time of the attack. Yet another study investigated state prisoners with five or more convictions. The investigation showed that four out of five of these prisoners were regular drug users.

"Eighty percent of the cops shot in this area were shot because people were high on drugs," states Joe Arpaio, sheriff of Maricopa County, Arizona (which includes the city of Phoenix). To Arpaio and others, the link between drug use and crime is obvious, and fighting one problem automatically helps in the fight against the other. "Drug control is crime control," concludes former New York City mayor Rudolph Giuliani.

Drug War backers further argue that drug users are more likely than nonusers to abuse their children and their spouses.

The Rockefeller Laws

The War on Drugs began as a get-tough effort, designed to put drug felons behind bars for many years. Nowhere was the effort tougher than in New York State. In the 1970s, New York governor Nelson Rockefeller and state lawmakers were frustrated with escalating heroin use in New York City. They passed the nation's strictest drug laws, known as the Rockefeller laws. The laws included mandatory minimum sentences. For instance, a conviction for possession of 4 or more ounces (113 g) of heroin or cocaine carried a mandatory minimum sentence of fifteen years in prison. Judges had no authority to hand out lesser sentences, no matter what the circumstances.

Over the years, critics began to charge that the laws were too harsh, frequently landing first-time and small-scale drug offenders in jail for many years. New York lawmakers revised the laws in 2004 to eliminate the strictest provisions. In 2009 state legislators and Governor David Paterson finally dismantled the decades-old laws. They passed legislation that repealed many of the mandatory minimum sentences and gave judges the ability to send first-time, nonviolent offenders to drug treatment programs instead of jail. The legislation provided funds for more drug courts and treatment programs. It also allowed some drug offenders in prison to apply to have their sentences commuted, or reduced.

Above: Nelson Rockefeller took a strong antidrug stance while he was governor of New York.

They might also endanger people by driving under the influence of drugs. Public health specialists estimate that drugged driving is almost as prevalent as drunken driving—and can be just as deadly. In one study, the National Highway Safety Administration examined fatal car crashes in seven states. The data revealed that about 18 percent of drivers tested positive for commonly abused drugs, including prescription drugs.

HOW TOUGH IS TOO TOUGH?

The authorities—and society as a whole—want to see violent drug offenders behind bars. That certainly makes sense from a standpoint of public safety. But Drug War critics claim that U.S. prisons are crowded with *nonviolent* drug offenders. "We have . . . tens of thousands of cells, hundreds of thousands of cells, being occupied by nonviolent drug offenders," claims retired police chief Norm Stamper.

Below: A large number of fatal car crashes are the result of drugged or drunk driving.

Once again, Drug War supporters disagree. They say that in fact U.S. prisons aren't packed with nonviolent drug offenders. The DEA explains that nonviolent drug users are much more likely to end up in treatment programs than in jail. According to the DEA, judges in Ohio "offer treatment to virtually 100 percent of first-time drug offenders and over 95 percent of second-time drug offenders." The agency says that "99 percent of [Ohio] offenders sentenced to prison had one or more prior felony convictions or multiple charges." Drug court programs, which send first-time drug offenders to treatment instead of prison, are expanding throughout the nation. Some states are also moving drug offenders to treatment facilities after initially sending them to prison.

But opponents of the Drug War don't accept these statistics without a fight. They say that many sentences for nonviolent drug offenders are still too harsh. Consider the case of New Yorker Miguel Arenas. An air force veteran with no prior run-ins with the law, Arenas was arrested for selling 2 ounces (57 g) of cocaine in 1992 and sentenced to fifteen years in prison. Wheelchair-bound Jimmy Montgomery smoked marijuana to relieve muscle spasms caused by his spinal cord injuries. In 1992 he received a ten-year prison sentence for possession of 2 ounces of marijuana with intent to distribute it.

Drug War critics say that such sentences are inexcusably severe. They say there's no point in keeping people like Arenas and Montgomery locked up in prison. These punishments only destroy their future, without making society any safer. "We need to reserve those jail spaces, those cells, for people who are certifiably dangerous, those who have made it clear that they don't belong among the free in our society, because they're simply too dangerous," says Norm Stamper.

As for the drug court system, Drug War opponents agree that it's a step in the right direction. But they note that drug court programs are available to fewer than half of U.S. drug offenders, and those who drop out of the programs can still be sent to jail.

More places turning to drug courts

From the Pages of
USA TODAY

Damon Fuseyamore vividly recalls smoking "my last nickel [five dollars' worth] of crack" on June 16, 1997, while sitting on the steps outside his New York City residence. He said he owed loan sharks money and had been arrested two weeks before "with six nickels of crack and a bunch of money."

He was charged with selling crack and was looking at two to seven years in prison. But he had another option.

"I had a choice of doing jail time or changing my life and going through treatment," he said. "If you have a choice between doing two-to-seven or going through the program and going into treatment, any smart person would take the program."

Fuseyamore, 45 and the father of a 10-year-old son, celebrated 10 years of sobriety in June and has been a mechanic for the New York City Fire Department for six years, according to Dennis Reilly, former director of the Brooklyn Treatment Court. Fuseyamore's story is one of thousands touted by supporters of alternative drug courts.

The courts, which are multiplying across the USA, began 18 years ago as an experiment to attack a growing crack cocaine epidemic in Miami. They rely on treatment, rigorous supervision and accountability as a way to help, for the most part, non-violent drug users rather than sending them to prison.

There are now 2,016 drug courts in about 1,100 counties, according to the National Drug Court Institute. That number, the institute says, is up from 1,048 five years ago and is nearly 1,800 more than existed 10 years ago.

According to West Huddleston, CEO of the institute, a 2005 study—the most recent available—showed 70% of drug court participants graduate from the program and reoffend at a rate of 17% on average, compared with the 66% recidivism rate of drug offenders who do time in prison.

Above: In Illinois some drug offenders attend special drug rehab programs.

That study also showed the annual average cost of a drug court participant is $3,500, compared with annual prison costs that range from $13,000 to $44,000 per inmate, Huddleston said.

Supporters say more is needed. "We're scratching the surface. I think it's critical that a drug court is in every county in America," said Huddleston, who estimates that 120,000 people are served annually by drug court alternatives, but potentially 4 million more people could benefit by such programs.

—David Unze

> " **I think it's critical that a drug court is in every county in America.**

—**WEST HUDDLESTON**, NATIONAL DRUG COURT INSTITUTE
USA TODAY · DECEMBER 21, 2007

FOLLOW THE MONEY

Finally, Drug War critics often say that antidrug efforts are a waste of taxpayer dollars. They say that the billions spent pursuing and punishing drug users each year are better spent elsewhere. We should spend the money on education and health care, they say, or on locking up truly dangerous people, such as murderers and rapists.

According to Drug War supporters, this argument is flimsy. Consider the numbers. The federal government spends almost $20 billion dollars each year on drug control. That sounds like a lot of money, and it is. But when you consider that the entire U.S. budget for 2008 was $2.98 trillion, the drug budget suddenly doesn't look so big after all. And Drug War advocates say that this money is all well spent. Roughly 55 percent goes toward law enforcement, while the remaining 45 percent goes to drug treatment and prevention.

Are drug prevention and drug treatment a waste of taxpayer money? Certainly, even the most ardent critics of the

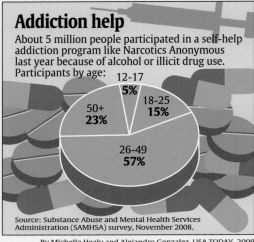

USA TODAY Snapshots®

Addiction help

About 5 million people participated in a self-help addiction program like Narcotics Anonymous last year because of alcohol or illicit drug use. Participants by age:

- 12-17 **5%**
- 18-25 **15%**
- 50+ **23%**
- 26-49 **57%**

Source: Substance Abuse and Mental Health Services Administration (SAMHSA) survey, November 2008.

By Michelle Healy and Alejandro Gonzalez, USA TODAY, 2009

Drug War would not argue against spending money to treat drug addicts and warn young people away from the dangers of drugs. But it's the law enforcement side of the equation that most disturbs Drug War opponents. When they look at efforts to fight drug cartels, drug dealers, and drug users, they see nothing but waste and futility.

Drug War opponents—specifically those who promote drug legalization—envision an entirely different framework. They see a scenario in which police officers do not pursue and punish drug users or drug traffickers. They envision a world in which drugs are legal and highly regulated. Let's examine what this sort of world might look like.

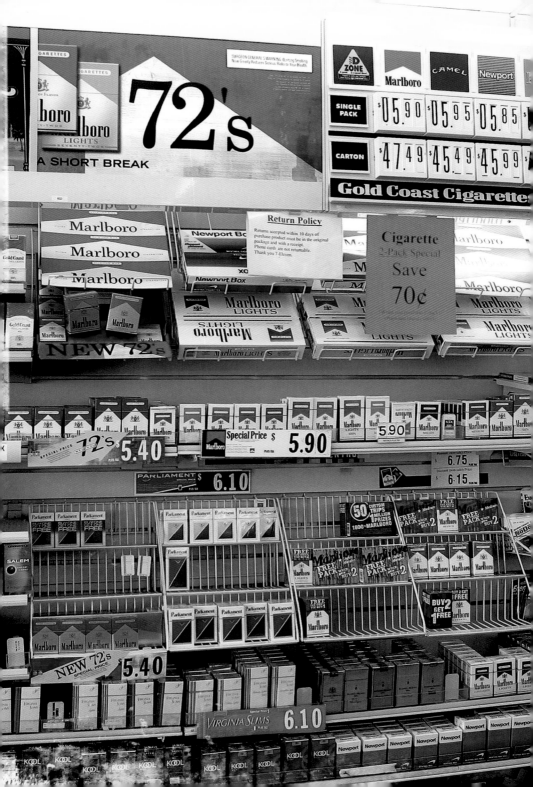

CHAPTER FIVE

The Potential of Legalized Drugs

WHEN PEOPLE FIRST HEAR ABOUT THE IDEA OF legalizing drugs, they usually have many questions. They ask: Does this mean you'd be able to buy Ecstasy at the corner store? Would you be able to order marijuana along with a café latte at a coffee shop? Would you need a doctor's prescription to buy drugs or a government permit? Who would sell the drugs, and how much would they cost? What role would the government play in regulating drug sales?

Many people also worry when they hear about legalized drugs. They say: drugs can be dangerous—do we really want to make them more readily available?

These are all good questions, and those who promote drug legalization don't have all the answers or details. They don't even agree on the answers among themselves. But they all say that with a well-thought-out system of legalization, drugs would be safer, drug-related violence would decline, and the government

Left: Adults can buy tobacco and sometimes alcohol at convenience stores. Why can't they buy other kinds of drugs?

would save a lot of money. They even think that overall drug use might decline under legalization.

DANGER ZONE

Drugs can be harmful to the user's health. Those who advocate legalizing drugs don't dispute that. Studies show that Ecstasy can cause heat stroke, dehydration, increased heart rate and blood pressure, anxiety, and other psychological symptoms. Cocaine use can cause increased heart rate and blood pressure, paranoia, and cardiac arrest (heart attack). Methamphetamines and LSD can cause psychological damage.

Health problems multiply when people become addicted to drugs—using them more frequently and in larger quantities. Some drugs, such as heroin, cause the most agony when people try to withdraw from, or stop using, them. People trying to kick a heroin addiction often experience pain, insomnia, vomiting, terror, and other symptoms.

Death is obviously the worst-case scenario in drug use. The famous 1960s rock and rollers Janis Joplin, Jimi Hendrix, and Jim Morrison all died of drug overdoses. Many other celebrities, including singer Elvis Presley and actor Heath Ledger, died of prescription drug overdoses.

The dangers of drug use extend beyond the specific drugs that people put in their bodies. Often intravenous (IV) drug users share syringes to inject drugs. In this way, they often also share blood, some of which gets inside the syringes during injection. HIV/AIDS, hepatitis C, and other illnesses can be spread through shared blood, and IV drug users are frequently afflicted with these illnesses.

Legalization proponents do not deny the health risks of drug use. They do not want to encourage people to use harmful drugs. They also agree with drug enforcement organizations that Americans need education to keep them off drugs and treatment programs to help them quit drugs if they do get hooked. But pro- and anti-legalization forces

Left: Actor Heath Ledger died of an accidental prescription drug overdose in 2008. *Right:* Radio talk show host Rush Limbaugh admitted to addiction to prescription drugs in 2003. He was arrested on charges related to his drug use in 2006.

disagree on how to achieve these goals. Whereas anti-legalization forces say that law enforcement is a key part of the antidrug equation, pro-legalization forces say that law enforcement is part of the problem.

Pro-legalization forces also say that their opponents approach the drug issue with too broad of a brush. Government and other antidrug agencies argue that all drug use is harmful to health, that even occasional use can lead to addiction, and that all drug use is wrong. Pro-legalization forces want the government to take a more nuanced approach. They say that millions of Americans use drugs without becoming addicted and with no long-term health damage. They say that the person who has the occasional marijuana cigarette is no more of an addict than the person who has the occasional cocktail after work. And the person who tries cocaine at a party is probably endangering his or her health less than someone who regularly smokes tobacco cigarettes, they argue.

Needle Exchanges and Harm Reduction

When IV drug users share syringes to inject drugs, they might also share blood and bloodborne diseases, such as HIV and hepatitis C. More than 1.5 million Americans have contracted HIV/AIDS since the epidemic began in the early 1980s. About one-third of these people contracted HIV through IV drug use or by having sex with an IV drug user.

Studies show that access to clean syringes can reduce HIV and other bloodborne infections among IV drug users. Many organizations operate needle exchange programs, which give new, sterile syringes to IV drug users and dispose of dirty ones safely.

Above: At needle exchange programs, drug users can trade dirty needles for clean ones. Dirty needles can spread HIV/AIDS and other diseases.

Some needle exchange programs also refer drug users to drug treatment programs, health services, and other social services.

Efforts to provide clean needles to drug addicts are part of a movement called harm reduction. Backers say it's unrealistic to expect to eliminate all drug use. They say that as long as some people will always use drugs, society must find ways to help them and to reduce the harm caused by their drug use. Needle exchange programs are a key component of harm reduction efforts.

Despite the success of needle exchanges, not all of them operate legally. In some parts of the United States, owning, distributing, and selling syringes for nonmedical use is a crime. Syringes are considered drug paraphernalia (equipment). Their prohibition is intended to cut down on illegal drug use. In some places, police officers have arrested needle exchange workers and clients and have shut down exchange programs.

Groups such as the Drug Policy Alliance are working to change the laws, so that needle exchanges can operate legally nationwide. They stress that people's lives are at stake. HIV/AIDS can be a killer, especially for those without access to expensive medical treatments. DPA would even like to see the federal government fund needle exchange programs as a way to control the spread of HIV.

Many people oppose needle exchange programs. Critics say the programs encourage IV drug use and send the message that drug use is okay, as long as it's done with clean equipment. They especially don't want to see the federal government involved in needle exchange programs. In many ways, the controversy over needle exchanges echoes the controversy over legalized drugs. Will legalizing syringes and making them freely available lead to increased drug use? Will it end up costing lives instead of saving them? The answers are not clear.

It's true that drugs *can* harm health—but when used infrequently they usually don't. Remember presidents Clinton and Obama. They both used drugs briefly as young men and did not suffer long-term health damage. Neither man became a drug addict. And those who do become addicts, legalization proponents say, need help not punishment.

MAKING DRUGS SAFER

Proponents of drug legalization say that if people do choose to use drugs, it's important that the drugs be as safe as possible. And drug prohibition, they explain, only adds to the dangers of already dangerous drugs.

Once again, legalization forces make a comparison to Prohibition. During the 1920s, many Americans made illegal moonshine and bathtub gin at home. The home brewers used anything they could get their hands on—antifreeze, rubbing alcohol, and embalming fluid—to make intoxicating drinks. The ingredients were sometimes poisonous and so was the resulting liquor. In the most infamous case, about fifty thousand Americans became paralyzed after drinking a Prohibition-era ginger beer called Jake.

In modern times, drug producers make similarly poisonous concoctions. Drug dealers often cut, or dilute, their

> ❝ **Whether you call it legalization, decriminalization or drug policy reform, the bottom line is that [it] . . . would put more drugs into the hands of our children and make drugs more available on our nation's streets.** ❞

—**BARRY MCCAFFREY,** FORMER DRUG CZAR
◆ USA TODAY · OCTOBER 6, 1999

Above: A customs officer checks the purity of seized heroin. Dealers routinely mix heroin with other, cheaper substances.

products with a variety of powders and chemicals. In this way, they make their drug supplies go further. Some of the ingredients dealers use to dilute drugs are more dangerous than the drugs themselves. Others are relatively harmless. LEAP's Jack Cole explains that most heroin users know that a bag of heroin won't be 100 percent pure. In fact, the typical bag will contain 40 percent heroin and 60 percent cutting agent. But sometimes dealers don't mix their products well. A user might unknowingly get a bag of heroin that is 80 percent pure. The user injects what he or she thinks is a normal dose but gets twice as much of the drug as expected. This "hot shot" is an overdose and often will kill the drug user.

Cole believes that it is drug prohibition that leads to this kind of death. Drug dealers—working outside the law, with no government regulation—routinely sell adulterated products that are much more dangerous than the drugs on their own. If drugs were legalized, Cole explains, the government could set rules about their manufacture. Licensed drugmakers would have to list product ingredients on drug packages. The government could also require manufacturers to print health warnings, similar to the surgeon general's warning on packages of cigarettes. If people still chose to buy drugs, at least they would know what they were buying, how potent the drugs were, and the health risks involved. Under such a scenario, negative side effects and drug overdoses would probably decline. Remember that when alcohol became legal again after Prohibition, people no longer got sick or died from drinking poisonous moonshine.

CUTTING OUT THE CARTELS

Proponents also say that drug-related violence would likely decline with legalization. Yet again, they point to Prohibition. When the United States banned

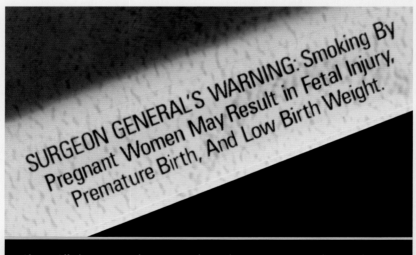

Above: All cigarette packages must have the surgeon general's warning printed on them. If drugs were to be legalized, they would need to carry similar warnings about the dangers of drug use.

Above: The Saint Valentine's Day Massacre shocked Chicago in 1929. When Prohibition ended, gang violence dropped sharply.

liquor sales in 1920, gangsters moved in to sell liquor illegally. The result was murder and mayhem on the streets of many big cities. In the most gruesome incident, members of Al Capone's gang gunned down seven members of Bugs Moran's gang in the 1929 Saint Valentine's Day Massacre in Chicago.

When selling liquor became legal again in 1933, the gangsters got out of the bootlegging business. Some moved on to other illegal ventures, such as gambling and prostitution. Others went legit. They moved into the once-again-legal liquor industry, paid business taxes, and followed government regulations. The repeal of Prohibition put an end to gangland-style killings within the liquor industry because liquor dealers no longer fought one another for control of markets and distribution systems. Instead, people operated distilleries, breweries, liquor stores, and nightclubs within the confines of the law. They settled any business disputes through the courts.

N.M. governor calls for drug legalization

From the Pages of
USA TODAY

New Mexico Gov. Gary Johnson told activists and scholars Tuesday that the government should regulate narcotics but not punish those who abuse them.

The maverick Republican, whose stance on legalizing drugs has angered lawmakers, spoke at a conference on national drug policies at the Cato Institute, a libertarian think tank here. Johnson said legalization remains a viable alternative to a federal program that has spent billions but done little to stem drug use. It was his most detailed explanation yet of how legalization of drugs might work.

"For the amount of money we're putting into the war on drugs, I suggest it's an absolute failure," Johnson said. "Make drugs a controlled substance like alcohol. . . . Legalize it, control it, regulate it, tax it. If you legalize it, we might actually have a healthier society."

Johnson's remarks only stoked the controversy that has enveloped him since he began calling this summer for a national dialogue on drug policy that included the ideas of legalizing or decriminalizing drugs.

Last week, he took an even bolder stance, saying he supported legalizing illicit drugs. Though Minnesota Gov. Jesse Ventura also has said the government should regulate illegal drugs, Johnson is the highest-ranking elected official to push for such a strategy on a national level.

Barry McCaffrey, President Clinton's drug czar and a retired general, said in a statement Tuesday that Johnson's ideas are misguided. He says he plans to speak Thursday in Albuquerque in opposition to Johnson's drug plan. "Whether you call it legalization, decriminalization or drug policy reform," he said, "the bottom line is that the agenda espoused by people like Governor Johnson would put more drugs into the hands of our children and make drugs more available on our nation's streets."

The federal Office of National Drug Control Policy contends that policies are working. The number of people using cocaine dropped 69% from 1983 to 1998. And the number of youths using cocaine dropped 13% between

1997 and 1998, according to Bob Weiner, a spokesman for McCaffrey.

Johnson suggested a host of new laws that would accompany a policy of legalization, such as the prohibition of drug sales to people under 21 and a provision that would allow employers to issue drug tests and fire an employee caught using narcotics on the job.

Driving or committing a crime under the influence of drugs could lead to stiffer punishments, he said, the same way using a gun or driving drunk bring harsher penalties.

Above: Governor Gary Johnson appears on a TV show to discuss his views on drug decriminalization.

Johnson's views on drugs have made headlines before. During his first gubernatorial campaign in 1994, Johnson acknowledged that he used marijuana and cocaine while he was a student at the University of New Mexico. But the 46-year-old triathlete says he didn't touch drugs after college and has not even had a drink in the past 12 years.

"I'm not pro-drug. . . . I stopped because it is a handicap," he said. He also said that if he and his friends had been caught, they would not have deserved a prison term. "I don't think we can continue to lock up [Americans] because of bad choices."

—Charisse Jones

Proponents say the same thing would happen if drugs were legalized. Big pharmaceutical companies might get into the narcotics business. Tobacco companies might start selling marijuana.

What would happen to the cartels and street drug dealers under such a scenario? Drug Policy Alliance head Ethan Nadelmann predicts that these criminals would choose one of four paths. Some would go straight. They would become legal sellers of drugs. Others might continue to sell drugs illegally—operating a black market in competition with legal dealers. Still others would switch to different criminal activities. Finally, some would get out of both the drug business and the crime business altogether. They would pursue different, legal business ventures.

At first, the criminals might give the legitimate sellers some serious competition. But Nadelmann predicts that, in the long run, the big companies would come to dominate the drug business. Going head-to-head with established firms, black marketers would no longer be able to reap huge profits from illegal drugs sales. Their businesses would probably not disappear altogether but would certainly shrink greatly.

With the criminals sidelined, drug selling would become like any other legal enterprise, legalization proponents say. Firms would obey government laws and regulations. Since they wouldn't be breaking the law, drug sellers wouldn't need to run from or do battle with the police or drug enforcement agents. Staff members of law-abiding companies wouldn't shoot one another on city streets. When they had disagreements, they would settle them through the U.S. legal system.

Of course, not all drug-related crime would disappear under this scenario. In any legalization program, drugs would be off-limits to those under the age of twenty-one. Some black marketers would still try to sell drugs to children, and the police would need to pursue and arrest them. In addition, the police would need to keep people from driving under the influence of drugs and committing other drug-related crimes.

But proponents say that most violent crime associated with drug prohibition would decline greatly if drugs were legalized. Terry Nelson is a LEAP member and a former agent with the U.S. Border Patrol, the U.S. Customs Service, and the U.S. Department of Homeland Security. He believes that drug violence would shrink under legalization, both in the United States and other nations. "Ending drug prohibition is the only sure-fire way to end the cartel violence that is terrorizing El Paso's sister city of Ciudad Juárez and others across Mexico," Nelson says.

As an added bonus, the government could tax the newly legal drug businesses, adding great amounts of money to government coffers. Instead of spending billions of dollars a year on tracking down drug offenders, the government would come out ahead—with billions of dollars in new tax revenues.

Below: Emergency responders help a pedestrian hurt by drug dealers in Ciudad Juárez, Mexico, in late 2008.

NEW PRIORITIES

Drug legalization would certainly have a dramatic impact on the nation's court system. With legalization, police officers, district attorneys, and judges would have more than 1 million fewer cases to handle each year. Not prosecuting drug offenders would also free up space in the nation's overcrowded state and federal prisons.

The financial savings would be vast. Consider that it can cost more than forty thousand dollars of taxpayer money to keep someone in prison for a year. Suppose we put that money elsewhere—into drug treatment programs, for example. A year in a residential drug treatment program costs much less than a year in prison, and the results are certainly better. Studies show that treatment programs frequently help people stay off drugs long term, whereas prison rarely does.

Proponents again acknowledge that legalizing drugs wouldn't eliminate the need for all drug enforcement. Any legalization system is going to have rules and regulations about drug sales and drug use—just as we have rules and regulations about alcohol sales and use. Some people are still going to abuse the system and break the law. Some people will certainly still end up in jail for drug crimes. But under a system of legalization, the law-abiding drug user will not face punishment. And instead of chasing and punishing drug users, the police and courts can focus their efforts elsewhere.

GET REAL

Let's not kid ourselves. Although some people use drugs briefly and move on, others go down the wretched path of drug addiction. In his book *Beautiful Boy*, writer David Sheff tells a wrenching story of his son's descent into methamphetamine addiction. Sheff's son Nic stole from his employer and his parents to get money to buy drugs. Once a bright and promising student, Nic dropped out of college. He ended up living on the streets in San Francisco. He traded sex for drugs and drug money. He risked HIV infection by sharing

Above: Nic Sheff and his father, David, pose for a photo in 2008. The father and son team were promoting their drug-related memoirs.

dirty needles with other drug users. Nic's father persuaded him to enter a drug rehab program. But as soon as Nic finished the program, he started using drugs again. He entered one program after another but was unable to stay off drugs for long. (In 2006 Nic finally managed to kick his addiction. He remains drug-free in 2009.)

Nic's story is sadly a typical one. At meetings of Narcotics Anonymous—an international association of recovering drug addicts—one can hear story after heartbreaking story of lives ruined by drugs: children neglected and abused, jobs lost, marriages crumbled, and health destroyed. After hearing these stories, some people might wonder why anyone would consider legalizing drugs. Won't taking away the penalties for drug use simply create more users, more addicts, and more ruined lives?

Legalization proponents don't take addiction lightly. They recognize its dangers and want to prevent it as much as anyone else. Although acknowledging that no one can read the future, they predict that drug use would not rise with legalization. Surveys show that people who shun drugs will continue to shun them, even if they are legal. A 2007 poll by the Zogby organization asked, "If hard drugs such as heroin or cocaine were legalized, would you be likely to use them?" Ninety-nine percent of the 1,028 respondents answered no. Only 0.6 percent said yes, and the remaining 0.4 percent said they weren't sure.

Some advocates say that legalization might actually reduce drug use. First of all, taking away the fear of punishment and prison might encourage some drug users to "come out of the closet." They will no longer have to hide their drug use and might seek drug treatment programs voluntarily.

Legalization might also take away the "forbidden fruit" effect in drug use. Professor Doug Husak explains: "Many people—adolescents in particular—are attracted to an activity precisely *because* it is forbidden or perceived as dangerous. Much of the thrill of illicit drug use stems from its illegality and the culture of deviance that surrounds it. . . . Might the use of some illicit drugs actually decrease because they are no longer forbidden?"

To make the case for legalization, proponents frequently point to the Netherlands. In that European nation, people over the age of eighteen can buy marijuana in coffee shops. They can smoke the marijuana in the

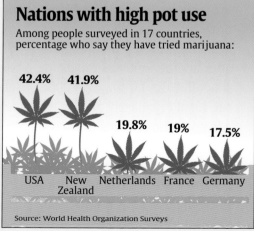

USA TODAY Snapshots®

Nations with high pot use

Among people surveyed in 17 countries, percentage who say they have tried marijuana:

42.4%   41.9%   19.8%   19%   17.5%

USA   New Zealand   Netherlands   France   Germany

Source: World Health Organization Surveys

By Anne R. Carey and Alejandro Gonzalez, USA TODAY, 2008

Above: This coffee shop in Amsterdam, the Netherlands, sells marijuana. Adults in the Netherlands can buy and smoke the drug without fear of prosecution.

shop or take it home. Has this system turned the Netherlands into a nation of out-of-control marijuana smokers? The statistics say no. According to one survey, 28 percent of tenth graders in the Netherlands have tried marijuana. In the United States, where marijuana is illegal, 41 percent of tenth graders have used it.

LEAP's Jack Cole explains that the Netherlands' approach has neutralized the forbidden fruit effect. "Children in the Netherlands know that when they reach the age of 18 they can go in a coffee shop and get all the marijuana they want," he explains, so they're not particularly excited about sneaking marijuana ahead of time. The nation's

Legalization Case Study: Portugal

In 2001 the European nation of Portugal took a bold step in drug policy. It became the first nation in modern times to abolish punishments for drug use. Under Portuguese law, a person found with small amounts of heroin, cocaine, methamphetamines, or any other drug is not punished. Instead, the authorities refer that person to a drug treatment program, although he or she is not required to attend. The law still punishes drug dealers, drug traffickers, and those who commit drug-related crimes.

Portugal changed its laws in part as a cost-saving measure. Locking people up in prison is much more expensive than paying for their drug treatment. The government also wanted to encourage users to come forward and seek treatment. When drugs are illegal, many addicts keep their drug use hidden. Legalization allows drug users to confront their drug problems without fear of punishment.

Critics worried that Portugal's law would only worsen the nation's drug problems. But the opposite appears to be true. In a 2009 study, the Cato Institute found that between 2001 and 2006, drug use dropped slightly among teenagers in Portugal. Rates of HIV infection from needle sharing dropped significantly, while the number of Portuguese people requesting drug treatment more than doubled. In addition, Portugal was able to save money on law enforcement, freeing up more funds for drug treatment and prevention programs. Law officers were also able to focus more energy on apprehending large-scale drug dealers.

minister of health concludes, "I think what we have done in [the Netherlands] is we have managed to make pot boring."

No matter what system a nation uses—whether drugs are legal or illegal—some people are still going to become drug addicts. Proponents of legalization say those people should be treated compassionately, not punished. Under legalization, with less money going to punishing drug users, more funds would be available for programs to treat drug addiction. With strict medical supervision, clinics might even distribute free drugs to carefully wean addicts down to lower doses and then off drugs completely. (Some U.S. clinics already use this approach with heroin addicts.)

Everyone agrees that keeping people off drugs in the first place is the ideal solution to the U.S. drug problem. How do we best do that? Proponents of legalization say that threats of punishment are not the right method. They say that education is key. Jack Cole makes an interesting comparison to cigarette smoking. Smoking is legal in the United States and always has been. In 1965, 42 percent of U.S. adults smoked cigarettes. By then scientists knew that cigarette smoking was deadly. Public health officials began a massive campaign to reduce the

number of smokers in the United States. But the government didn't make smoking illegal or arrest smokers. Instead, it used education to teach people about the dangers of tobacco use. The program worked. By 2007 only about 20 percent of U.S. adults smoked tobacco. This example shows that we can reduce the use of dangerous drugs using education, not punishment.

HOW WOULD IT WORK?

In the United States and many other nations, you can walk into a supermarket or drugstore and buy liquor. You can buy cigarettes there too. As long as you show identification proving that you're old enough (eighteen for cigarettes and twenty-one for alcohol), you're free to buy as much booze and tobacco as you want. Would the same be true of legalized drugs? Would you be able to buy them at your neighborhood store?

Probably not. Most people who support legalization say that this supermarket model is a bad idea. They don't want to encourage drug use or make it

Above: Even under a system of legalization, drugs would probably not be freely available in stores the way alcohol is.

too easy for people to get drugs. Ethan Nadelmann has written about what he calls the right-of-access model. Under this model, adults would be able to order small amounts of any drug by mail. The drugs would come from reputable suppliers and would be safer than current street drugs. The government would set the rules and regulations about the quantity and quality of drugs available for purchase.

Other advocates call for legalizing marijuana and not other drugs—similar to the system used in the Netherlands. Still others want drug trafficking and drug dealing to remain illegal but want drug use alone to be legal. This is the system used in Portugal, and studies show that it has actually reduced drug use in that nation. Another option is to keep drug use illegal but not to send users to jail, only to mandatory treatment programs.

> ❝ **When dealing with drugs and addictions, offenders need treatment and second chances, not knee-jerk, lock-'em-up policies.** ❞
>
> —**ETHAN NADELMANN,** EXECUTIVE DIRECTOR, DRUG POLICY ALLIANCE
>
> $USA TODAY · JULY 9, 2007

Advocates stress that no system would involve a big drug-taking free-for-all. Under any legalization model, officials would have to establish strict penalties for driving under the influence of drugs or selling drugs to children. Employers might still choose to drug-test workers and punish those who used drugs. The drug laws and restrictions would be similar to those established for drinking and selling alcohol. People arrested for drug-related crimes—such as stealing money to buy drugs—might still end up in jail, but simple drug use itself would not be a crime.

The next question after "How would it work?" is "Would it work?" Would U.S. society really function well under a system of drug legalization, or would our problems—including crime, violence, and addiction—only get worse? Many people say that drug legalization would make things *much* worse. Their arguments follow.

CHAPTER SIX

The Risks of Legalized Drugs

MANY PEOPLE REJECT THE DRUG LEGALIZATION arguments. They believe that legalizing drugs will increase drug use and all the social ills that accompany drug use. With legalized drugs, they say, more people will drive drugged, use drugs on the job, commit drug-related crimes, and become addicted to drugs. And more drug-using parents will neglect or abuse their children.

Legalization advocates believe that laws have very little to do with whether or not people use drugs. But opponents argue that drug laws in fact provide important barriers to drug use. Remember Charles Van Deventer, the writer we met in chapter 4? He says that drug laws saved him from addiction. He was afraid of being arrested, and that fear helped him give up his drug use. Legalization opponents agree with Van Deventer. They say that by taking away the fear of punishment, legalizing drugs will

Left: This mother and daughter used drugs on a regular basis. They ended up living on the streets.

open the floodgates to drug abuse and drug addiction. "Americans feel up to their hips in drugs now," writes William Bennett, drug czar under President George H. W. Bush. "They would be up to their necks under legalization."

FADE TO BLACK

Legalization advocates envision a world where drug sales are taxed and regulated. They say that once legal businesses get into the drug market, the black market for drugs will shrink—and much drug-related violence will disappear as well. Legalization opponents say this is a fantasy world. They don't think drug cartels and traffickers will simply shut up shop if big pharmaceutical and tobacco companies enter the drug market.

Consider the gun business. Every day in the United States, law-abiding gun manufacturers and dealers buy and sell guns. They pay taxes on this business and follow all government regulations. For instance, the government requires gun

dealers to perform computer background checks to make sure that customers don't have criminal records. Has this system of taxation and government regulation eliminated the black market in guns? Certainly not. Across the United States, thousands of people buy and sell guns illegally. They smuggle guns across the U.S.–Mexico border; sell guns to teenagers, criminals, and others who aren't supposed to own them; and break other gun-control laws. They certainly don't report their sales to the authorities or pay taxes on them. The black market in guns is a multibillion-dollar business that exists alongside the legal gun business.

Comparisons to the drug market are obvious. Even with a system of legalized drugs, the black market would still operate, many argue. Opponents of legalization say that black marketers would still try to sell drugs to kids. They would ignore government regulations about drug purity, safety, licensing, and taxation. They might be able to sell drugs more cheaply than the legal businesses, because they would not incur the cost of taxes or quality control, and their cheaper drugs would attract more buyers. Under a legalization scenario, opponents say, the government would still need to hunt down the black market dealers, even as it was trying to regulate and monitor the legal drug businesses.

Are these predictions correct? That's the problem with the legalization debate. Nobody knows for sure how economic forces would shift under a legalization scenario. Proponents of legalization make comparisons to the black market in alcohol, which dried up after the end of Prohibition. Opponents make comparisons to the modern black market in guns, which thrives alongside legal gun sales. Without a crystal ball to read the future, nobody knows for sure which side is correct.

Below: Black markets don't always disappear when products become legal. These guns, confiscated by police officers in 2009, were bought on the black market.

The Terror–Drug Connection

The terrorist attacks in the United States on September 11, 2001 (9/11), focused new light on the international drug trade. The attacks were the work of al-Qaeda, an Islamist terrorist organization based at the time in Afghanistan. Al-Qaeda operated in alliance with the Taliban, another Islamist organization. The Taliban had taken control of Afghanistan in the mid-1990s.

Afghanistan is one of the world's major suppliers of opium, which is made into heroin. Al-Qaeda controls much of

Above: A farmer checks his poppy crop in Afghanistan. Poppies are used to produce opium. Farmers can make much more money growing poppies than growing other crops.

Afghanistan's heroin trade. It has used vast profits from this trade to finance terrorism, such as the 9/11 attacks.

Following 9/11, the United States invaded Afghanistan to fight both the Taliban and al-Qaeda. Working with a newly installed Afghan government, the United States tried to shut down the Afghan heroin trade. At home in the United States, the Office of Drug Control Policy ran television ads that warned Americans that by using drugs, they were supporting terrorism.

As in Latin America, the U.S. government has tried to persuade Afghan farmers to switch from growing opium poppies to growing grain and other food crops. But farmers can earn ten times more money growing poppies than other crops, so the Afghan heroin trade continues.

Besides al-Qaeda, other terrorist organizations use drug trafficking to finance their operations. In Colombia a terrorist group called the FARC is a major drug trafficker. In Peru a group called the Shining Path controls many drug operations.

Opponents of the Drug War say that legalizing drugs might actually reduce terrorism, just as it might reduce crime. Under a system of legalization, they argue, law-abiding companies would take over the Afghan opium trade. Manufacturers could use the opium to make morphine and other important painkilling drugs. Some terrorist groups might continue to deal in opium illegally, but their control over the market would be broken. Their drug operations and profits would probably decrease greatly, some say. Others disagree. They say that legalizing drugs would only increase the drug trade, without making a dent in terrorist groups' drug profits.

THE WRONG ROAD

Economic arguments aside, opponents of legalization say that drug use is simply wrong. They say that all drugs have the potential to damage a user's health and to damage society as a whole. If the government were to legalize drugs, it would essentially be sending the message that drug use is okay, opponents say. They say the government should never send that message, because in fact drug use is not okay.

A system of government legalization and oversight might also mislead the public. Suppose drugs were legal, and a young person picked up an Ecstasy tablet at a party. If the tablet came from a well-known pharmaceutical company, the teenager might think the drug was safe. After all, it had been manufactured according to government rules. It had been bought and sold legally. It came from a sterile pill bottle with the ingredients listed on the label. The teenager might naturally think that the tablet was no more harmful than a bottle of beer.

But opponents of legalization want kids to know that Ecstasy *isn't* safe, no matter who manufactures it or sells it. Again, opponents of legalization want the public—especially kids—to realize that drug use can be harmful, even deadly.

By this point, astute readers might have noticed the contradictions in U.S. drug policy. They might ask, why is it legal for adults to buy alcohol and not drugs? After all, alcohol can be deadly too. In fact, alcohol kills more Americans every year than all drug use combined. Alcohol can be dangerously addictive. Excessive drinking can damage a person's liver, kidneys, and other organs. Drunken drivers cause about thirteen thousand traffic deaths each year. Alcoholic parents frequently neglect and abuse their children. Alcoholic workers often can't do their jobs safely and responsibly. Given that alcohol is so damaging, why do we allow people to buy it freely when we prohibit marijuana, heroin, cocaine, and other mind-altering drugs? If we're going to allow people to

Above: Opponents of drug legalization want teenagers especially to know that drugs are not safe.

drink as much as they want, shouldn't we allow them to use as many drugs as they want?

Opponents of legalization have sensible answers to these questions. Yes, they confirm, alcohol use can be dangerous and deadly. Alcohol use does cause untold heartache to millions of Americans each year. But would we really want to multiply that heartache by making drugs legal too? Do we really want more impaired workers—whether that impairment is due to drugs or alcohol? Do we really want more people driving under the influence of mind-altering substances? Do we really want more drug-related abuse and violence? Billions of dollars worth of law enforcement, educational programs, and treatment programs can't keep some Americans from driving and going to work drunk.

Growing danger: drugged driving

From the Pages of USA TODAY

It happened in an instant.

Ohio Highway Patrol Trooper Leonard Gray had stopped to direct traffic around a jackknifed truck in December 2002 when a car, traveling about 50 mph, hit him. Gray, 53, was flipped into the air, his head crashed into the car's windshield and he landed—unconscious, with his legs broken and head bloodied—on the pavement.

The driver who hit Gray, 61-year-old Ronald Hamrick, had been convicted of drug possession previously and had cocaine in his system when he was tested seven hours after the accident, Hocking County assistant prosecutor David Sams says.

More than 1.5 million people were arrested in the USA last year for driving drunk. Police departments and public health specialists estimate that at least as many people drive under the influence of drugs each year—and rarely are prosecuted for it.

Now, in an effort that is similar to the movement that began inspiring anti-drunken-driving laws a quarter-century ago, a growing number of government and law enforcement officials are pressing for laws that target drugged driving.

Congress, encouraged by White House anti-drug czar John Walters, is considering proposals that would use the lure of federal transportation money to push states to adopt what Sams wants in Ohio: "zero-tolerance" laws that would make it a crime for anyone to drive with any amount of illicit drugs in their system.

The Drug Policy Alliance, the Marijuana Policy Project and other groups that push for more liberal drug laws say they agree that people should not drive when they're high. But the groups say that the push for zero-tolerance laws is misguided and unfair because it would punish people for private behavior rather than for actions that harm others, such as driving impaired.

The groups say, for example, that the proposed laws could ensnare a recreational drug user who smokes marijuana at a party on a Friday and still has residues of the drug in his urine when he drives to work Monday—without showing any sign of being impaired.

The critics say that police could use zero-tolerance laws to target types of drivers, particularly young adults, whom the police believe are most likely to use drugs. And, the critics say, the proposed laws would have no effect on people who become impaired on legal drugs such as prescription tranquilizers or over-the-counter cold medicines.

"They are going to end up taking people with a Grateful Dead bumper sticker and dragging them down to the [police] station for a drug test," says Bill Piper, national affairs director for the Drug Policy Alliance, a non-profit based in New York City. "It's just a matter of time before they say you have to pass a drug test before you can get a driver's license."

Walters counters that authorities have to draw the line somewhere, and that a simple, clear guideline—like that used to determine alcohol intoxication—is needed to combat drugged driving. And besides, Walters says, drugs such as cocaine and marijuana are illegal, so a driver who tests positive likely has broken the law.

Using U.S. Census data and Monitoring the Future, a national survey of high school students conducted in 2003 by the University of Michigan, the White House anti-drug czar's office concluded that one in six high school seniors had admitted to having driven while they were high on drugs.

[National Highway Safety Administration official Richard] Compton says that in one study of fatal crashes in seven states, researchers tested drivers for about 50 commonly abused substances. They found that more than half the drivers had used alcohol and about 18% had used drugs.

Gray, who is still recovering from his injuries, says that governments must go beyond new laws to educate the public and make drugged driving unacceptable in the same way it became unfashionable to drive drunk.

"It scares me because it seems like the kids are not afraid" of driving high, says Gray, who was a trooper for 25 years before he had to retire on disability because of the accident. "They are more willing than ever to try the drugs. They don't drink. They won't try cigarettes because they know all about lung cancer. [But] they don't seem to know it's not a joke to drive on drugs."

—Donna Leinwand

Prohibition Revisited

Most historians agree that Prohibition didn't work. The vast majority of Americans were unhappy with the law. It was nearly impossible to enforce. It led to violence, corruption, and in some cases death (either by gang violence or by poisonous liquor).

But opponents of drug legalization point out that in some ways, Prohibition *did* work. Outlawing liquor actually did cause Americans to drink less. Consider these statistics. From 1916 to 1919, right before Prohibition started, Americans drank on average 2 gallons (7.4 liters) of alcohol per person per year. During the years of Prohibition, although some people drank more, overall drinking dropped by about 40 percent—to about 1.2 gallons (4.5 liters) per person per year. Once Prohibition was repealed in 1933, U.S. drinking began a steady climb back upward.

Clearly, outlawing liquor sales during Prohibition caused less drinking. Drug legalization opponents say that outlawing drugs does the same thing. They explain that drug laws provide a barrier to access to drugs and help keep down total drug use in the United States.

What makes us think that under a system of drug legalization we'd have any more success keeping Americans from driving and going to work under the influence of drugs?

And what about all those billions of law enforcement

> **Make drugs a controlled substance like alcohol. . . . Legalize it, control it, regulate it, tax it.**

—NEW MEXICO GOVERNOR GARY JOHNSON
USA TODAY · OCTOBER 6, 1999

> **Addiction is so pernicious [destructive] it often takes incarceration [imprisonment] for an addict to confront the havoc in her life. The addicts I interviewed credited the strong arm of the law and intense therapy for their . . . sobriety.**
>
> —AMY HOLMES, CONSERVATIVE COMMENTATOR
> **USA TODAY** · MARCH 30, 2001

dollars we'd supposedly save if drugs were legalized? It's true that we wouldn't have to spend that money arresting and locking up casual drug users. But we would have to spend that money to pay for the social ills of increased drug use, opponents of legalization say. We'd need to put more social workers on the job to attend to drug-related domestic violence. We'd need more police officers to chase down drugged drivers. Daniel Lungren, former attorney general of California, believes "the costs in homelessness, unemployment, welfare, lost productivity, disability payments, school dropouts, lawsuits, medical care costs, chronic mental illness, accidents, crime, child abuse, and child neglect would all increase if we in fact legalized drugs." In the end, opponents say, nothing would be gained by legalizing drugs and much would be lost.

CHAPTER SEVEN

Is Marijuana Different?

WHEN MICHAEL PHELPS WAS PHOTOGRAPHED smoking from a bong, the Kellogg's cereal company came down hard, canceling his endorsement contract. But most Americans—especially young people—shrugged at the news that the Olympic swimmer might have smoked marijuana with friends. After all, one in three adult Americans admit to having tried marijuana at least once. Twenty-five million Americans say they smoked marijuana within the past year.

And these users are far from the fringe element of society once associated with marijuana use. President Barack Obama and New York City mayor Michael Bloomberg have both admitted to past marijuana use. "You bet I did," replied the mayor when asked if he had ever smoked marijuana, "and I enjoyed it."

It's against the law to smoke marijuana in the United States, but many people think it shouldn't be. Most people—even full-scale Drug War opponents—agree

Marijuana comes from the hemp plant *(left)*. Many people think marijuana is far less dangerous than other drugs.

that methamphetamines, cocaine, and heroin can be deadly. But many Americans say that marijuana is different. They say it's much safer than other drugs—and that it can even be used as medicine. They say that any move to legalize drugs in the United States should begin with marijuana.

RULES AND REGULATIONS

The U.S. government doesn't agree that marijuana is a harmless or beneficial drug. In fact, the government places marijuana on its list of "Schedule 1" drugs. These are drugs that:

- Have a high potential for abuse
- Have no accepted medical use
- Are not safe for use under medical supervision

Other Schedule 1 drugs include heroin, Ecstasy, and LSD. Drugs classified as Schedule 1 are not sold in pharmacies. Doctors cannot prescribe them to patients. Buying and selling these drugs is completely illegal under U.S. law.

The government has four additional schedules (2 through 5) for drugs that have some medical benefits but that might be abused or addictive. For example, the addictive but painkilling drug morphine is a Schedule 2 drug. The occasionally abused anxiety drug Xanax is a Schedule 4 drug. With certain restrictions, doctors can prescribe

Illegal drug use

People 12 and older who say they have illegally used the following drugs during the past month:

Marijuana	14.6 million
Prescription drugs	6 million
Cocaine (non-crack)	1.5 million
Inhalants	600,000
Methamphetamine	600,000
Crack cocaine	500,000
Ecstasy	500,000
Heroin	200,000
LSD	100,000

Source: Substance Abuse and Mental Health Services Administration, 2004 National Survey on Drug Use and Health

By Adrienne Lewis, USA TODAY, 2006

drugs from schedules 2 through 5 drugs and pharmacies can sell them.

The government says that marijuana harms users' health and has no medical benefits, and therefore it belongs in Schedule 1. Marijuana advocates disagree. They say marijuana is safe when used infrequently and even helpful to some sick people. Which group is right? Let's look at the arguments.

HAZARDOUS TO YOUR HEALTH

Marijuana comes from the flowers, stems, seeds, and leaves of the hemp plant, also known as cannabis. Most people use marijuana by smoking it. Some people mix it into food.

The psychoactive chemical in marijuana is tetrahydrocannabinol, or THC. When THC enters the brain, the marijuana user starts to feel euphoric, or high. Most people enjoy the experience, but occasionally marijuana makes people feel anxious, depressed, distrustful, or fearful.

THC affects the brain and body in several ways. Short-term effects include memory loss, distorted perception, trouble with thinking and problem solving, diminished motor skills, and increased heart rate. With regular marijuana use, these short-term effects can create longer-term problems for users at school or work. For example, studies show that high school marijuana smokers score much lower on standardized tests than their non-marijuana-smoking classmates. "Marijuana impacts young people's mental development, their ability to concentrate in school, and their motivation and initiative to reach goals," explains the DEA.

The long-term effects of marijuana smoking mirror those experienced by tobacco smokers. Some studies show that heavy marijuana smokers are susceptible to respiratory illnesses; lung infections; and cancer of the lungs, mouth, throat, and esophagus. Studies also show that marijuana smoke can contain more than twice as many cancer-causing chemicals as cigarette smoke. Other studies have linked marijuana to

Hemp: Past and Future

Hemp is a useful plant. For thousands of years, people have made textiles, rope, paper, and other products from the strong fibers of the hemp plant. Hempseed oil has been used to fuel lamps and lubricate machinery. People have made food from both hempseeds and hempseed oil.

Hemp was once a common crop in the United States. U.S. presidents George Washington and Thomas Jefferson grew hemp on their farms. The crop remained a mainstay of U.S. agriculture until the mid-twentieth century.

When the Federal Bureau of Narcotics launched its war on marijuana in the 1930s, hemp came under fire. Certain varieties of hemp have high concentrations (between 3 and 20 percent) of the psychoactive chemical THC. People grow these varieties for marijuana. But "industrial hemp"—hemp used to make paper, textiles, food, and other products—has very low concentrations of THC (less than 1 percent). Nevertheless, when the U.S. government outlawed marijuana in the mid-twentieth century, it also outlawed industrial hemp. Once a common crop, industrial hemp disappeared from U.S. farms. In the process of fighting marijuana growers, drug enforcement agents uprooted and destroyed any industrial hemp plants they encountered.

additional health problems, including heart attacks and a weakened immune system.

Marijuana is not as addictive as many other drugs. The person who quits marijuana will not undergo the painful physical symptoms and cravings that people experience when they try to stop using heroin, for example. But some people do become dependent on marijuana for their emotional well-being. They become fixated on getting the drug, use it in large quantities, and feel uncomfortable without it. Each year, about 150,000 Americans enter rehab programs

Above: This rope is one of many products that can be made from hemp.

In modern times, many Americans think industrial hemp should again be made legal. They note that industrial hemp is legal in many nations, where it is made into various products. Since it has an extremely low THC content, it can't be used as a recreational drug. Advocates also note that hemp could be used to fight many environmental problems. For instance, making paper from hemp requires fewer toxic chemicals than making paper from wood. Hemp is naturally resistant to both pests and weeds. Therefore, farmers can grow hemp without using the many harmful pesticides and herbicides needed to grow other crops. Many people think hemp should be grown as a biofuel—or fuel made from plant material. Biofuels are better for the environment than fossil fuels such as coal, crude oil, and natural gas.

But reintroducing hemp would require a change in U.S. policy. The federal government contends that all hemp plants contain some THC. Therefore hemp, like marijuana, is illegal. Growing hemp remains against federal law in the United States.

to get treatment for marijuana dependency.

Like many other drugs, marijuana harms more than just the user. Experts agree that marijuana does not make people violent. But the marijuana-using driver might not be able to judge distances properly; react quickly to road signs, traffic signals, or other vehicles; or concentrate on driving. The results can be deadly. In a 1990 study of 182 fatal truck accidents, the National Transportation Safety Board found that 12.5 percent were caused by drivers using marijuana.

MORE GOOD THAN HARM

With all these facts about health risks, who would possibly argue for legalizing marijuana? Actually, a lot of people argue that marijuana can be used safely and responsibly. Sure, marijuana use has health risks, but so do alcohol and cigarette use. The United States has laws that govern where, how, and at what age people can legally use alcohol and smoke cigarettes. Why not pass similar laws for marijuana use?

The leading group in the fight to legalize marijuana is the National Organization for the Reform of Marijuana Laws (NORML). On its website, NORML makes a thoughtful case for allowing people to own and use marijuana without criminal penalties. Many of the arguments echo those for legalizing all drugs. For instance, NORML argues that under a system of marijuana legalization, users would know that the drugs they purchased were safe. Buyers and sellers would pay taxes on their transactions, which would add money to government coffers (between $2 and $6 billion annually, according to one study). And legal marijuana sellers could use their business savvy to compete in the marketplace, thereby shrinking the black market and the crime and violence that accompanies it.

NORML stresses that under a legalization scenario, marijuana would remain off-limits to kids. And driving cars or operating heavy machinery under the influence of marijuana would still be illegal. But adults who used marijuana peacefully, without bothering anyone else, would not be breaking the law. They wouldn't fear the police. They wouldn't answer to judges, serve time in jail, or enter court-supervised rehab programs. They wouldn't have criminal records dogging them after a drug conviction.

The police arrest more than seven hundred thousand Americans each year on marijuana offenses. About 86 percent of the offenders are arrested for simply possessing marijuana, not selling it. Legalization advocates see a great benefit if seven hundred thousand fewer drug cases worked their way through the U.S. legal system each year. They say that police and courts could focus instead on arresting and punishing murderers and other violent criminals. They say that society would be better off for it.

NORML and other legalization advocates admit that marijuana isn't 100 percent harmless. But in the grand scheme of things, they say, its health risks are minimal. And when compared to other drugs, marijuana is downright tame. Every year, cigarettes and tobacco kill people by the thousands. Cigarettes alone kill more than four hundred thousand people each year. People regularly overdose on cocaine, heroin, methamphetamines, and other drugs. But health officials can't identify one case of a person overdosing on marijuana or dying due to marijuana use alone.

Furthermore, legalization advocates say that the notion of "marijuana addiction" is overblown. Kicking a marijuana habit is only slightly more difficult than giving up coffee, they claim. They say that treatment programs for so-called marijuana addicts are filled with people who were given a choice by the court: go to treatment or go to jail. Naturally, most people choose the treatment route, but that hardly makes them addicts.

NORML and other groups don't present these arguments to encourage marijuana use. They simply do so to illustrate their belief that marijuana is not

> **[Legalization] would end the needless harassment of individuals who peacefully and privately use marijuana.**
>
> —*LAS VEGAS REVIEW-JOURNAL*
> USA TODAY · AUGUST 27, 2002

Whose Data Are Correct?

Trying to get a handle on the marijuana debate can be frustrating. Antidrug groups say that marijuana is dangerous, addictive, and a gateway to harder drugs. Drug-policy reform groups say the opposite is true. Each side cites scientific studies and statistics. The problem is, different studies frequently come to different conclusions.

If you visit "Marijuana: The Facts," a Web page created by the Drug Policy Alliance, you'll find the following statement: "There have been no reports of lung cancer related solely to marijuana, and in a large study presented to the American Thoracic Society in 2006, even heavy users of smoked marijuana were found not to have any increased risk of lung cancer." The DPA says it's a myth that marijuana is more harmful to the lungs than tobacco.

If you visit "Exposing the Myth of Smoked Medical Marijuana: The Facts," a DEA Web page, you'll find this information: "According to the National Institutes of Health, studies show that someone who smokes five joints per week may be taking in as many cancer-causing chemicals as someone who smokes a full pack of cigarettes every day."

This information poses quite a dilemma. The DPA says the DEA's facts are myths. The DEA says the DPA's myths are facts. Which group should we believe? Should we assume the government is always right? Should we believe everything that doctors and scientists say? There are no easy answers.

nearly as bad as the government makes it out to be.

A GATEWAY DRUG?

People sometimes call marijuana a "soft" drug, because it is not as dangerous as many other illegal drugs. But some people believe that marijuana is a gateway to "hard" drugs such as heroin and cocaine. Studies show that very few people use heroin or cocaine without first trying marijuana. One study from the National Institute on Drug Abuse says that those who have used marijuana are 104 times more likely to use cocaine than those who have never used it.

Proponents of the "gateway theory" explain that marijuana lowers a user's fears and inhibitions about drug use, emboldening him or her to try harder drugs. Marijuana also exposes users to a "drug culture"—one in which using illegal drugs is celebrated.

If you listen to frequently told tales from Narcotics Anonymous meetings and rehab centers, the gateway theory seems to be correct. Methamphetamine addict Nic Sheff started his drug use with marijuana, and his experience is not uncommon. Michael Winerip, reporting on marijuana laws for the *New York Times*, recalls "stories in our little suburb about classmates of my kids smoking pot [marijuana] in middle school, using heroin in college, going into rehab, relapsing, trying again."

Proponents of the gateway theory say the government must do everything possible to stop marijuana use—especially

Above: A man rolls a marijuana cigarette. Many people see marijuana as the first step into the criminal drug culture.

among teenagers—so more serious drug problems don't occur. They predict that legalizing marijuana would inevitably lead to more users of hard drugs.

But many people reject the studies and arguments that support the gateway theory. Critics explain that just because most hard drug users *start* with marijuana, marijuana itself does not *cause* people to move on to harder drugs. After all, most hard drug users also start out drinking alcohol, but that doesn't mean alcohol is a gateway to hard drug use or that we should outlaw alcohol.

Opponents of the gateway theory explain that most people who experiment with drugs never go beyond marijuana. "Of the seventy million Americans who smoked pot in 1994," writes Judge Rudolph Gerber in *Legalizing Marijuana*, "98 percent did not wind up on anything harder than martinis. Only a tiny fraction went on to become heroin or cocaine addicts."

It's true that marijuana users are sometimes exposed to a world of hard drugs and drug dealers, but NORML says that marijuana prohibition is to blame. People who want to use marijuana have no choice but to buy it from the black market, since there is no legal market. If people could buy drugs from legal sources, similar to the coffeehouses in the Netherlands,

> " Is marijuana a gateway drug? That question has been debated since the time I was in college in the 1960s and is still being debated today. There's just no way scientifically to end that argument one way or the other. "

—**HARRISON POPE,** BIOLOGICAL PSYCHIATRIST

USA TODAY · FEBRUARY 6, 2007

NORML says, they would not be forced into a world of hard drugs, dishonest drug dealers, and sometimes, violence.

MARIJUANA AS MEDICINE?

People have used marijuana as medicine since ancient times. In 2737 B.C., Chinese emperor Shen Neng recommended marijuana tea to treat gout, rheumatism, and malaria. Queen Victoria, who ruled Great Britain from 1837 to 1901, took a marijuana tincture to ease the pain of menstrual cramps. In the United States, a reference book called the *United States Pharmacopoeia* lists all medications approved by doctors and the U.S. government. Marijuana was included in the book from 1850 to 1942.

Harry Anslinger, who headed the Federal Bureau of Narcotics from 1930 to 1962, made sure that the *Pharmacopoeia* no longer listed marijuana. Anslinger was convinced that marijuana was a killer drug, not a medicine. When the U.S. government drew up its five-category drug schedules in 1970, marijuana was assigned Schedule-1 status (no medical value and a high potential for abuse).

For the rest of the century, the Drug War took the spotlight. Presidents and other public officials denounced illegal drugs, including marijuana. But

Above: A Montana woman inhales medicinal marijuana in 2007 to help with symptoms from a brain tumor.

other forces were working behind the scenes. While publicly decrying marijuana use, the federal government did its own research on medical marijuana. It even dispensed marijuana to about thirty-five patients. This Compassionate Investigational Drug Program, started in 1978, permitted states to set up similar programs, although very few state programs got off the ground.

In 1982 the National Academy of Sciences (created by Congress to advise the government on scientific matters) released a report on the medical effects of various drugs. This report said that marijuana posed no danger to the human brain or nervous system. It further stated that marijuana had "shown promise in the treatment of a variety of disorders," including glaucoma (an eye disease), asthma, and the nausea and vomiting caused by chemotherapy (a cancer treatment).

By then marijuana use was a growing problem in U.S. schools. President Ronald Reagan had no interest in a report that touted the medical benefits of marijuana. Such a report might send the message to young people that marijuana use was okay—and in the eyes of the president, parents, and many in the public, marijuana use was not okay. The president dismissed the report as inaccurate.

Meanwhile, the Compassionate Investigational Drug Program continued to operate, but politicians thought that it too sent the wrong message about marijuana. President George H. W. Bush shut down the program in 1992.

But the medical marijuana movement would not go away. In 1996 voters in California approved the creation of medical marijuana programs for seriously ill patients. Organizations opened marijuana dispensaries. There, with a doctor's recommendation, sick people could buy marijuana for medical use.

The California medical marijuana dispensaries operated in violation of federal law, and the DEA soon moved to shut them down. In the 2000s, drug enforcement agents raided some medical marijuana dispensaries and made arrests. Agents even arrested some

Above: Medical marijuana stores popped up in California after passage of a proposition that okayed marijuana use for severely ill patients.

extremely ill marijuana users. But the state program continued to operate. Meanwhile, additional states defied federal law and created their own medical marijuana programs.

THE GOVERNMENT SAYS NO

Since the mid-twentieth century, the federal government has taken a strong stance against medical marijuana. According to the DEA:

> The Institute of Medicine conducted a comprehensive study in 1999 to assess the potential health benefits of marijuana and its constituent [chemicals]. The study concluded that smoking marijuana is not recommended for the treatment of *any* disease condition. In addition, there are more effective medications currently available. For those reasons, the Institute of Medicine concluded that there is little future in smoked marijuana as a medically approved medication.

More states move toward allowing medical pot use

From the Pages of USA TODAY

Some states are moving to legalize the use of marijuana for medical purposes in response to the Obama administration's decision to limit prosecutions of sick people or caregivers who use or dispense the drug.

Attorney General Eric Holder said last week that his agents will seek criminal charges only when both state and U.S. laws are violated. That signaled a shift from the Bush administration, whose agents raided several centers that dispense marijuana in California, where state law permits its

Above: DEA agents raid a medicinal marijuana club in San Francisco, California, in 2005. In 2009 the U.S. attorney general said the DEA would limit such raids.

medical use. Twelve other states also allow medical marijuana, but U.S. law prohibits its use for any reason.

"The change in the federal government's attitude . . . speaks volumes," says New Hampshire state Rep. Evalyn Merrick, a Democrat. She is the author of a bill that would legalize medicinal use of marijuana if approved by a doctor. It passed the state House on Wednesday, 234–138.

Merrick, a cancer survivor who once got relief from nausea by smoking pot, pushed a similar bill three years ago, but it failed. This year it is getting a warmer reception, and now heads to the Senate.

Holder's announcement boosts state proposals for changing marijuana laws, says Bill Piper, national affairs director for the Drug Policy Alliance, which advocates legalizing marijuana. "The politics around marijuana are changing," he says.

Sen. Chuck Grassley, an Iowa Republican who co-chairs the caucus on international drug control, says Holder is violating his oath of office if he fails to enforce federal marijuana laws. "Marijuana is a gateway to higher drugs," Grassley says.

Among states considering more relaxed laws:

- New Jersey. State Sen. Nicholas Scutari, a Democrat, in January introduced a bill that would permit medical use of marijuana. It passed the Senate last month and its prospects are good in the House, Scutari says.
- Illinois. A medical marijuana bill, introduced by state Rep. Lou Lang, a Democrat, is on the floor in both the House and Senate.
- Minnesota. State Sen. Steve Murphy of the Democratic-Farmer-Labor Party reintroduced a medical marijuana bill this year after its failure last year. It passed a House panel Wednesday, 9-6.

In November, Michigan and Massachusetts voters adopted marijuana laws. Massachusetts reduced penalties for possessing less than an ounce of marijuana to tickets and a $100 fine.

"The message it sends to young people is that it's not a big deal to use marijuana," says David Capeless, president of the Massachusetts District Attorneys Association. "That's the wrong message."

—Donna Leinwand

The federal government does not dispute that some ingredients in marijuana, namely THC, have some medical benefits. But the government says it makes no sense to administer these ingredients via smoke. After all, the tar and chemicals in marijuana smoke put people at risk for respiratory illnesses and lung cancer. Why would doctors treat their patients with cancer-causing chemicals?

Since 1985 doctors have been able to prescribe a drug called Marinol to their patients. Marinol contains synthetic, or human-made, THC. The Food and Drug Administration, which oversees drug safety in the United States, has approved Marinol to treat nausea and vomiting in cancer patients, appetite and weight loss in AIDS patients, and pain and muscle spasms in people with multiple sclerosis and other neurological disorders. The government says that Marinol is safe and effective, thus medical marijuana is not needed. The government also says that many conditions for which people smoke marijuana can be treated effectively without marijuana. For example, doctors have numerous treatments for glaucoma, including surgery.

But backers of medical marijuana say that approved medical treatments aren't always effective. Many patients say that Marinol offers them little relief. The drug takes more than an hour to take effect, whereas smoked marijuana offers relief

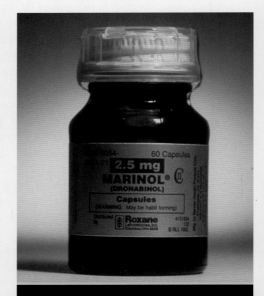

Above: Marinol is supposed to provide relief to severly ill patients just as marijuana does.

immediately. Patients also complain of unpleasant side effects with Marinol. Lastly, Marinol is much more expensive than marijuana. Pills can cost between six hundred and one thousand dollars per month. A patient would spend far less on a month's worth of medical marijuana.

COMPASSION OR CATASTROPHE?

Many Americans are outraged that the government has shut down medical marijuana dispensaries. Stephen Jay Gould was one of them. Before his death in 2002, Gould was a well-known scientist and science writer. He was also a cancer patient whose only relief from the nausea of chemotherapy treatments came from smoking marijuana. "It is beyond my comprehension . . . that any humane person would withhold such a beneficial substance from people in such great need," he wrote.

But former drug czar Barry McCaffrey presents the other point of view. "Just when the nation is trying its hardest to educate teenagers not to use psychoactive drugs, now they are being told that marijuana and other drugs are good, they are medicine," he laments. McCaffrey says there "could not be a worse message to young people" than doctors recommending marijuana to patients.

Some opponents of medical marijuana are less philosophical. They say that the whole medical marijuana movement is simply a front for recreational marijuana use. In California, where medical marijuana does not break state laws but does break federal laws, marijuana dispensaries have sprung up in Los Angeles and other cities. Some doctors write marijuana recommendations for patients complaining of common ailments, such as headaches or depression, when in fact the patients really want marijuana for recreational use. "It's really become a way of skirting the law for the recreational use of marijuana," says Los Angeles police lieutenant Paul Vernon, remarking on the flourishing medical marijuana shops in his city.

Above: Patients who use medical marijuana in California must have a doctor's recommendation and an ID card. Opponents of medical marijuana believe the system is too easy to exploit.

Proponents of medical marijuana see different hidden motives. They note that big pharmaceutical companies make vast profits by selling synthetic drugs to patients. If sick people instead smoked marijuana—which comes from a simple plant that can even be grown at home—drug industry profits would suffer. Medical marijuana advocates say that pharmaceutical companies are constantly working behind the scenes, pressuring lawmakers, and putting out anti–medical marijuana propaganda as a way to protect their own profits.

For many years, the U.S. government led the charge against medical marijuana. But under the Obama administration, that appears to be changing. In March 2009, Attorney General Eric Holder announced that the DEA would no longer raid medical marijuana dispensaries that were following state laws. The announcement signaled a major departure from the policies of the George W. Bush administration, which aggressively moved to shut down medical marijuana programs, regardless of state law.

Holder's announcement brought both cheers and jeers. The public remains split on the issue of medical marijuana, just as it remains split on the issue of legalized drugs in general.

END THE PRISON STATE
Legalize Pot Now!
Stop The Lies LEGALIZE!
America's Largest
STOP THE DRUG

CHAPTER EIGHT

Voice of
the People

MOST AMERICANS OPPOSE DRUG LEGALIZATION. Still, a significant number—more than one in four—think the idea has merit. In a 2008 Zogby poll, 27 percent of respondents supported legalizing drugs as the best way to solve the nation's drug problems.

When it comes to legalizing marijuana only, support goes much higher—and numbers have been rising. A 2009 ABC/*Washington Post* poll revealed that 46 percent of Americans supported legalizing small amounts of marijuana for personal use. In 1997, when the poll last asked that question, support was only 22 percent.

Experts think the rising numbers reflect changing demographics. In the late twentieth century, many older Americans were unfamiliar with marijuana. Particularly people born before 1946 had never tried it, and they feared it as much as they feared heroin or cocaine. The baby boom generation—those Americans born between 1946 and 1964—grew up during the

Left: Protesters march in support of legalizing marijuana in the United States. The number of Americans who support legalization of marijuana is rising.

133

counterculture years, when marijuana use exploded. These Americans, who have since reached middle age, are very familiar with the drug, might have tried it themselves, and don't fear it. Adults born after the baby boom are also very familiar with marijuana. This familiarity, coupled with studies on medical marijuana and the possible economic benefits of taxing marijuana, has won over increasing numbers of people to the legalization argument.

The Gallup organization has also conducted polls on legalizing marijuana. Gallup combined data from 2001, 2003, and 2005 to determine which groups of Americans are more likely than others to support legalization. The data confirm that younger Americans are more likely than older ones to support legalization. The data also show that nonchurchgoers are more likely than churchgoers to support legalization, Democrats are more likely than Republicans, college graduates are more likely than those without a college degree, and liberals are more likely than conservatives.

TAKING SIDES

Some of the Gallup data fits an expected pattern. The nation frequently splits along predictable lines on social and cultural issues such as drug use. The typical conservative American tends to vote Republican and tends to cherish traditional values, such as law and order and religious devotion. Conservatives also tend to have strong feelings about the difference between right and wrong, morality and immorality, and in their view, drug use is clearly wrong. Conservative political scientist James Q. Wilson declared, "Drug use is wrong because it is immoral and it is immoral because it enslaves the mind and destroys the soul."

The typical conservative view is that drug traffickers and drug users deserve punishment. To many conservatives, the idea of legalizing drugs is abhorrent. It represents surrender to forces that would corrupt children and undermine the fabric of society. This attitude has guided some of the get-tough policies of Republican administrations during the Drug War.

The liberal view is somewhat more forgiving. Liberals, who tend to vote Democratic, are more likely to view drug abuse as a social problem than a criminal one. Instead of punishing drug users, they say, society should help them with treatment and other social services. Liberals think the nation should also tackle the underlying factors that can lead to drug abuse—including poverty and joblessness.

But in the end, liberals and conservatives aren't that far apart in their attitudes about drugs. Even though liberals are more likely than conservatives to support the legalization of marijuana, the numbers aren't overwhelmingly in favor of legalization. Gallup polls reveal that 43 percent of liberals *did not* support legalization of marijuana in the early years of the twenty-first century, compared to 54 percent who did (the remaining 3 percent were undecided). And President Bill Clinton, a Democrat with liberal views on many social issues, was

Below: Both conservatives and liberals want to protect children from the destructive forces of drugs.

> " **The federal resources that have gone into the drug war have been heavily oriented toward police and incarceration [imprisonment] rather than treatment. We need to shift that use of resources.** "
>
> —**MARC MAUER,** THE SENTENCING PROJECT
> **USA TODAY** · MAY 28, 2009

just as fierce a drug warrior as the Republican presidents who immediately preceded and followed him (George H. W. Bush and George W. Bush). Conversely, the Republican administrations of the late twentieth and early twenty-first centuries were not focused solely on law, order, and the punishment of drug offenders. These administrations included funding for treatment and education as well.

Below: Drug offenders participate in a drug and alcohol counseling session in 2005. Treatment costs less than prison and helps many drug users quit for good.

In the end, the public is not greatly divided over issues of drug use and abuse. Most Americans agree that drug use is a negative and needs to be reduced. People disagree on the methods needed to achieve that goal, however.

THE NEXT STEP

The election of President Barack Obama came during a critical time in the Drug War. When Obama took office in early 2009, Mexican drug violence had reached alarming proportions, with about ten thousand killings in the prior two years. The Obama administration announced that it would fight the Mexican cartels with a combination of new technology at the border, increased coordination among U.S. and Mexican law enforcement agencies, and renewed emphasis on decreasing demand for drugs via education and treatment.

Some people wondered if marijuana legalization might also be part of President Obama's drug policy. The Obama administration's announcement that it would not raid medical marijuana dispensaries seemed to signal to some that the president might be open to the idea. But at an online town hall meeting in March 2009, the president put that notion to rest. A citizen had submitted a question: "With over 1 out of 30 Americans controlled by the penal system, why not legalize, control, and tax marijuana to change the failed war on drugs into a money making, money saving boost to the economy? Do we really need that many victimless criminals?"

> " [Marijuana] legalization isn't in the president's vocabulary, and it certainly isn't in mine. "
>
> —GIL KERLIKOWSKE, DIRECTOR OF THE WHITE HOUSE OFFICE OF NATIONAL DRUG CONTROL POLICY
>
> USA TODAY · MAY 21, 2009

New drug czar ready to corral forces

From the Pages of USA TODAY Drug czar Gil Kerlikowske says one of his top priorities is curtailing abuse of prescription drugs—such as the addictive painkiller OxyContin—which are readily available in the U.S.

"We get overly concerned about drugs coming in, but the pharmaceuticals are here already," he said in an interview Wednesday with *USA TODAY*.

He says he'll push for more states to adopt prescription-monitoring programs, databases in which doctors and pharmacists log prescriptions for addictive drugs so law enforcement can track them.

Kerlikowske, who became director of the White House Office of National Drug Control Policy on May 7, described drug abuse as a "public health problem." Yet the former Seattle police chief added, "That doesn't mean law enforcement doesn't have a role to play."

Above: Drug czar Gil Kerlikowske testifies about drug cartels in Mexico during a congressional hearing in Washington, D.C., in 2009.

He said he was stunned to learn recently that more people in the U.S. die from drugs than from gunshot wounds.

"We're going to shout that from the rooftops," he said. "We have a national effort to combat swine flu. In the same way, we can bring all forces to bear on the drug problem."

Kerlikowske said he supports courts that offer treatment instead of prison for addicts and federal funding for needle-exchange programs to stop the spread of disease.

His approach departs from that of the Bush administration, which heavily funded law enforcement task forces and advocated for tough sentences for drug offenders.

The Obama administration wants to make sentences for crimes involving crack cocaine the same as those for crimes involving powder cocaine. Currently, crack-related sentences are longer.

Attorney General Eric Holder also has limited prosecutions of sick people or caregivers who use or dispense marijuana for medical reasons. He has said his agents will seek criminal charges only when both state and U.S. laws are violated. During the Bush administration, agents raided several centers that dispense marijuana in California, where state law permits its medical use.

On his first trip outside Washington since assuming his new role, Kerlikowske told a law enforcement crowd attending a drug initiative conference Wednesday that marijuana should stay illegal, but public health officials—not police—should lead efforts to reduce illegal drug use.

"Legalization isn't in the president's vocabulary, and it certainly isn't in mine," he told 300 federal agents and law enforcement officials.

He sought to show strong support for law enforcement, making his first stop a 6:30 a.m. roll call at a Nashville Police Department precinct.

After speaking at the conference, Kerlikowske visited a drug court with a residential-treatment center. He also toured a residence for women with addictions who were recently released from prison.

"The state of Tennessee has built all the prison cells it needs" but has not invested enough in treating drug abusers, Criminal Court Judge Seth Norman, who runs the Davidson County Drug Court, told Kerlikowske.

The new drug czar agreed: "Rotating people in and out and through the system doesn't make a lot of sense."

—Donna Leinwand

The president's answer to the question was short: "The answer is, no, I don't think that is a good strategy to grow our economy." The president didn't provide any explanation for his stance, but his answer was not surprising. Despite growing support for marijuana legalization, a majority of Americans still oppose it. The president's opinion mirrored that of most voters.

Marijuana legalization seems unlikely in the near future—if at all. And the legalization of all drugs seems even more unlikely. Most of the public and most politicians oppose the idea. Most people aren't willing to take the chance on the increased drug use and drug addiction that might result from legalization.

What is likely in the near future is reform of many drug laws and Drug War tactics. President Obama has announced that he supports

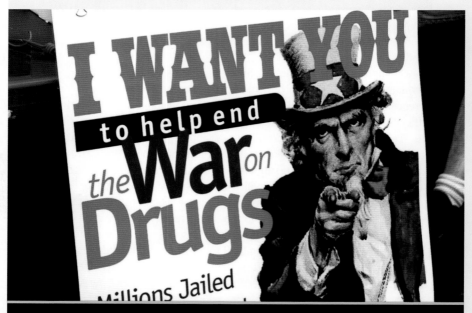

Above: A protester holds a sign condemning the Drug War. The Obama administration has moved away from the term *War on Drugs*, but the fight continues.

equal sentencing laws for crack and powdered cocaine users. The tough Rockefeller sentencing laws have been dismantled. Medical marijuana dispensaries can operate freely if they follow state laws. Even the phrase *War on Drugs* might be falling by the wayside. Obama's drug czar, Gil Kerlikowske, announced in June 2009 that he would no longer use the term. "When you talk about war, really the only tools you have to deal in war are force—and people also see it as a war on them, not a war on [drugs]," he explained.

By any name, the fight against illegal drugs appears to be shifting into new territory. With cartel violence on its southern border, the United States might also need some new strategies to win that fight. But no matter what strategies we use, no matter what the future antidrug efforts bring, people will probably keep asking: "Would it help if we legalized drugs?"

TIMELINE

1613	John Rolfe sends the first shipment of Virginia tobacco to England.
CA. 1800	Americans start forming temperance societies to fight for a ban on alcoholic beverages.
1861–1865	Doctors use morphine to treat soldiers wounded during the Civil War.
1886	John Pemberton invents Coca-Cola, which contains a small amount of cocaine.
1906	The Pure Food and Drug Act requires manufacturers to list ingredients on food and medicine labels.
1914	The Harrison Narcotics Act taxes and regulates the sale of opiates and cocaine.
1919	States ratify the Eighteenth Amendment, which bans the manufacture, transportation, and sale of liquor in the United States.
1920	Prohibition goes into effect.
1924	The Heroin Act makes it illegal to manufacture heroin in the United States.
1930	The U.S. government establishes the Bureau of Narcotics.
1933	States ratify the Twenty-First Amendment, which repeals Prohibition.
1937	The Marijuana Tax Act establishes extremely high taxes and strict licensing requirements for buying and selling marijuana.
1942	The *United States Pharmacopeia* drops marijuana from its list of approved drugs.
1960s	U.S. college students begin experimenting with marijuana and other drugs.

1972	The War on Drugs begins.
1973	The federal government creates the Drug Enforcement Administration. New York State passes the Rockefeller Drug Laws.
1982	The National Academy of Sciences releases a report listing the health benefits of marijuana.
1984	First Lady Nancy Reagan initiates the "Just Say No" campaign.
1985	The Food and Drug Administration approves Marinol, which contains synthetic THC, as a treatment for some health conditions.
1986	Congress passes the Anti-Drug Abuse Act.
1989	The first drug court begins, in Dade County, Florida.
1996	Voters in California approve medical marijuana programs for seriously ill patients.
1999	The Institute of Medicine says it does not recommend smoking marijuana as a treatment for any medical conditions.
2001–2008	The DEA raids medical marijuana dispensaries in California.
2002	The Office of National Drug Control Policy uses television ads to link drug use with terrorism.
2009	New York dismantles the last of the Rockefeller Drug Laws. Attorney General Eric Holder says the DEA will not raid medical marijuana dispensaries.

GLOSSARY

addiction: physical and emotional dependence on a habit-forming substance, such as alcohol or heroin

black market: a network of illegal buying and selling

cartel: a group of independent businesses that work together to control the market for certain products

drug courts: courts that sentence drug offenders to rehabilitation programs instead of prison

drug czar: head of the federal government's Office of National Drug Control Policy

gateway theory: the belief that marijuana use leads to the use of harder drugs

harm reduction programs: programs designed to reduce the harm caused by illegal drug use

Marinol: a government-approved drug containing synthetic THC, the psychoactive ingredient in marijuana

narcotics: drugs that can relieve pain or cause stupor, sleep, or coma, depending on the amount taken

opiates: drugs made from or containing opium. Opiates include morphine and heroin.

overdose: a toxic or deadly dose of a drug

Prohibition: the legal ban on the manufacture, transportation, and sale of alcoholic beverages in the United States. Prohibition lasted from 1920 to 1933.

rehabilitation: a program designed to help people break an addiction to drugs or alcohol

tetrahydrocannabinol: THC; the chief intoxicating ingredient in marijuana

SOURCE NOTES

9 Donna Leinwand, "Use of Ecstasy among Teens Is Up; Harder Drugs Are Becoming More Popular, Study Says," *USA TODAY*, November 27, 2000, A13.

12 Homer, *The Odyssey*, trans. Robert Fagles (New York: Viking, 1996), 131.

12 Prov. 31:6-7 (Revised Standard Version).

12 Ps. 104:15 (Revised Standard Version).

13 Wilbur F. Crafts, Mrs. Wilbur F. Crafts, Mary Leitch, and Margaret W. Leitch, *Intoxicating Drinks and Drugs in All Lands and Times* (Washington, DC: International Reform Bureau, 1911), 5.

18 Kurt Maier, "Inside the Library with Kurt Maier," *Journeys and Crossings*, 2009, http://www.loc.gov/rr/program/journey/lctour-transcript.html (June 7, 2009).

19 Hany Aly, "Preemptive Strike in the War on Pain: Is It a Safe Strategy for Our Vulnerable Infants?" *Pediatrics* 114, no. 5 (November 2004) : 1,335.

19 Department of Psychology, University at Buffalo, "Before Prohibition," Addiction Research Unit, 2001, http://wings.buffalo.edu/aru/preprohibition.htm (June 7, 2009).

23 Michael A. Lerner, *Dry Manhattan: Prohibition in New York City* (Cambridge, MA: Harvard University Press, 2008), 31.

23 Edward Behr, *Prohibition: Thirteen Years That Changed America* (New York: Arcade Publishing, 1996), 22.

25 Patrick Cox, "Learn from Prohibition," *USA TODAY*, October 15, 2002, A10.

27 Rudolph Gerber, *Legalizing Marijuana: Drug Policy Reform and Prohibition Politics* (Westport, CT: Praeger, 2004), 4.

28 Ibid., 5.

28 Ibid., 13.

29 Edward Hunting Williams, "Negro Cocaine 'Fiends' Are a New Southern Menace," *New York Times*, February 8, 1914, http://query.nytimes.com/mem/archive-free/pdf?res=9901E5D61F3BE633A2575BC0A9649C946596D6CF (June 7, 2009).

29 Robert Sabbag, *Snowblind: A Brief Career in the Cocaine Trade* (New York: Grove Press, 1998), 69.

29 Behr, *Prohibition*, 69.

29 Gerber, *Legalizing Marijuana*, 9.

31 Richard Lawrence Miller, *The Case for Legalizing Drugs* (New York: Praeger, 1991), 102.

32 Ibid.

35   Jack Kelley and LaBarbara Bowman, "Full-Court Press against Drugs," *USA TODAY*, August 16, 1989, A3.

39   Drug Enforcement Administration, *Speaking Out against Drug Legalization* (Washington, DC: Drug Enforcement Administration, 2003), 2.

43   Ross Colvin, "U.S. Drug Czar Named as Mexico Drug War Worsens," Reuters, March 11, 2009, http://www.reuters.com/article/joeBiden/idUSN11269402 (June 7, 2009).

47   Norm Stamper, "Citing Failed War on Drugs, Former Seattle Police Chief Calls for Legalization of Marijuana and All Drugs," interviewed by Juan Gonzalez and Amy Goodman, Democracy Now! March 30, 2009, http:www .democracynow.org/2009/3/30/citing_failed_war_on_drugs_former (June 7, 2009).

48   Rob Stewart, "Dorothy Gaines," Drug Policy Letter, 1998, http://www. drugpolicy.org/library/dp_letter_gaines2.cfm (June 7, 2009).

48   Jack A. Cole, *End Prohibition Now* (Medford, MA: Law Enforcement Against Prohibition, 2008), 1.

48   Dennis Cauchon, "Clinton Examines Clemency Cases; Groups Seek Release of Low-Level Drug Offenders," *USA TODAY*, December 22, 2000, A3.

51   Tony Newman, "War on Drugs Fails Black Americans," *USA TODAY*, October 19, 2005, A12.

53   Martin Torgoff, *Can't Find My Way Home: America in the Great Stoned Age, 1945–2000* (New York: Simon and Schuster, 2004), 429.

58   DPA Network, "Police, Drugs, and Corruption," Drug Policy Alliance, n.d., http://www.drugpolicy.org/docUploads/police_corruption_report.pdf (June 7, 2009).

62   Ted Galen Carpenter, *Bad Neighbor Policy: Washington's Futile War on Drugs in Latin America* (New York: Palgrave Macmillan, 2003), 171.

62   Cole, *End Prohibition Now*, 8

62   Ibid., 3.

63   Chris Hawley, "Clinton: U.S. Fueling Mexico's Drug Wars," *USA TODAY*, March 26, 2009, A6.

63   DPA Network, "Police, Drugs, and Corruption."

65   White House, "National Drug Control Strategy," Office of National Drug Control Policy, 2008, http://georgewbush-whitehouse.archives.gov/news/ releases/2008/03/national_drug_control_strategy_2008.pdf (June 7, 2009).

68   Charles Van Deventer, "I'm Proof: The War on Drugs Is Working," *Newsweek*, July 2, 2001, http://www.newsweek.com/id/78578/output/print (June 7, 2009).

70 Janet Kornblum, "Illicit Drug Use Down among Young," *USA TODAY*, September 5, 2009, A3.

70 Drug Enforcement Administration, *Speaking out against Drug Legalization,* 16.

70 Douglas Husak, *Legalize This! The Case for Decriminalizing Drugs* (London: Verso, 2002), 82.

72 Stamper, "Citing Failed War on Drugs."

73 Drug Enforcement Administration, *Speaking Out against Drug Legalization*, 24.

73 Stamper, "Citing Failed War on Drugs."

76 David Unze, "More Places Turning to Drug Courts," *USA TODAY*, December 21, 2007, A3.

84 Charisse Jones, "N.M. Governor Calls for Drug Legalization." *USA TODAY*, October 6, 1999, A4.

91 Terry Nelson, "Legalized Drugs Only Way to Halt Cartels," NAACP of Otero County, New Mexico, January 11, 2009, http://naacpoc.org/20009/01/13/legalized-drugs-only-way-to-halt-cartels/ (June 7, 2009).

94 StoptheDrugWar.org, "Poll: 99 Percent Wouldn't Use Hard Drugs If They Were Legal," StoptheDrugWar.org, 2007, http://stopthedrugwar.org/chronicle_blog/2007/dec/05/poll_hard_drug_legalization_little_use (June 9, 2007).

94 Husak, *Legalize This!*, 162.

95 Cole, *End Prohibition Now*, 11.

96 Ibid., 10.

99 Ethan Nadelmann, "Want to End the Drug Wars? Ditch Unreasonable Laws," *USA TODAY*, July 9, 2007, A10.

102 Husak, *Legalize This*, 151.

110 Jones, "N.M. Governor Calls for Drug Legalization."

111 Amy Holmes, "Pessimism Shouldn't Thwart War on Drugs," *USA TODAY*, March 30, 2001, A15.

111 Ibid., 153.

113 Michael Winerip, "Legalization? New for the Hard Question," *New York Times*, May 15, 2009, http://www.nytimes.com/2009/05/17/fashion/17generationb.html?hpw (June 7, 2009).

115 Drug Enforcement Administration, *Speaking Out against Drug Legalization*, 9.

119 John Ritter, "Measure Gambles on Marijuana," *USA TODAY*, August 27, 2002, A3.

120 DPA Network, "Marijuana: The Facts," Drug Policy Alliance, 2009, http://www.drugpolicy.org/marijuana/factsmyths/ (June 7, 2009).

120 Drug Enforcement Administration, "Exposing the Myth."

122 Gerber, *Legalizing Marijuana*, 71.

122 Rita Rubin, "CAUTION: Marijuana May Not Be Lesser Evil," *USA TODAY*, February 6, 2007, D1.

121 Winerip, "Legalization?"

124 Ibid., 36.

125 Drug Enforcement Administration, "Exposing the Myth of Smoked Medical Marijuana: The Facts," DEA, n.d., http://www.usdoj.gov/dea/ongoing/marijuana.html (June 7, 2009).

129 Gerber, *Legalizing Marijuana*, 84.

129 Ibid., 98.

129 William Welch, "L.A.'s Marijuana Stores Take Root," *USA TODAY*, March 8, 2007, A3.

134 Husak, *Legalize This*, 109.

136 Donna Leinwand, "Half of Men Arrested Test 'Positive' for Drugs," *USA TODAY*, May 28, 2009, A3.

137 Brian Montopoli, "Obama: Legalizing Pot Won't Grow Economy," CBS News, March 26, 2009, http://www.cbsnews.com/blogs/2009/03/26/politics/politicalhotsheet/entry4894639.shtml (June 7, 2009).

137 Donna Leinwand, "New Drug Czar Ready to Corral Forces," *USA TODAY*, May 21, 2009, A3.

140 Montopoli, "Obama: Legalizing Pot Won't Grow Economy."

140 Ina Jaffe, "Drug Czar Kerlikowske Leads Shift in Drug Policy," NPR, June 15, 2009, http://www.npr.org/templates/story/story.php?storyId=105393165 (September 1, 2009).

SELECTED BIBLIOGRAPHY

Behr, Edward. *Prohibition: Thirteen Years That Changed America*. New York: Arcade Publishing, 1996.

Carpenter, Ted Galen. *Bad Neighbor Policy: Washington's Futile War on Drugs in Latin America*. New York: Palgrave Macmillan, 2003.

Drug Enforcement Administration. *Speaking Out against Drug Legalization*. Washington, DC: Drug Enforcement Administration, 2003.

Gerber, Rudolph. *Legalizing Marijuana: Drug Policy Reform and Prohibition Politics*. Westport, CT: Praeger, 2004.

Husak, Douglas. *Legalize This! The Case for Decriminalizing Drugs*. London: Verso, 2002.

Miller, Richard Lawrence. *The Case for Legalizing Drugs*. New York: Praeger, 1991.

Miron, Jeffrey. *Drug War Crimes: The Consequences of Prohibition*. Oakland: Independent Institute, 2004.

Sheff, David. *Beautiful Boy: A Father's Journey through His Son's Addiction*. Boston: Houghton Mifflin Company, 2008.

Torgoff, Martin. *Can't Find My Way Home: America in the Great Stoned Age, 1945–2000*. New York: Simon and Schuster, 2004.

The Union: The Business behind Getting High. DVD. Toronto: Peace Arch Home Entertainment, 2007.

ORGANIZATIONS TO CONTACT

Drug Abuse Resistance Education (DARE)
P.O. Box 512090
Los Angeles, CA 90051
http://www.dare.com
In the DARE program, police officers teach schoolchildren how to resist peer pressure and live drug- and violence-free lives.

Drug Enforcement Administration (DEA)
8701 Morrissette Drive
Springfield, VA 22152
202-307-1000
http://www.usdoj.gov
The DEA is the federal agency charged with enforcing drug laws in the United States. In addition to law enforcement, the DEA offers resources on drug use prevention and treatment.

Drug Policy Alliance Network
70 West 36th Street, 16th Floor
New York, NY 10018
212-613-8020
http://www.drugpolicy.org
The Drug Policy Alliance Network promotes policy alternatives to the Drug War that are based on science, compassion, health, and human rights. It offers information on drug laws, drug abuse, and harm reduction.

Harm Reduction Coalition
22 West 27th Street, 5th Floor
New York, NY 10001
212-213-6376
http://www.harmreduction.org
HRC promotes the health and dignity of people and communities impacted by drug use. It aims to reduce the harm caused by overdose, addiction, and imprisonment for drug offenses. It also promotes needle exchange programs to reduce HIV and hepatitis C infection.

Law Enforcement Against Prohibition
    121 Mystic Avenue
    Medford, MA 02155
    781-393-6985
    http://www.leap.cc
    Made up of current and former members of law enforcement, LEAP
    believes that the government's Drug War has been ineffective and
    harmful and that society would benefit from the legalization and
    regulation of drugs instead.

Marijuana Policy Project
    P.O. Box 77492
    Washington, DC 20013
    202-462-5747
    http://www.mpp.org
    The MPP lobbies for legislation and ballot initiatives to allow medical
    marijuana use, a system of marijuana regulation instead of prohibition,
    and other changes in U.S. marijuana policy.

Narcotics Anonymous
    P.O. Box 9999
    Van Nuys, CA 91409
    818-773-9999
    http://www.na.org
    Narcotics Anonymous is an international association of recovering
    drug addicts. Participants meet weekly to share experiences and help
    one another live drug-free lives.

National Organization for the Reform of Marijuana Laws (NORML)
    1600 K Street NW, Suite 501
    Washington, DC 20006
    http://www.norml.org
    NORML believes that marijuana should be legal for recreational
    and medicinal use. It supports the creation of a legal market, with
    government-regulated producers and suppliers.

Office of National Drug Control Policy
    P.O. Box 6000
    Rockville, MD 20849-6000
    800-666-3332
    http://www.whitehousedrugpolicy.gov
    The ONDCP was established to create policies, priorities, and objectives
    for U.S. drug control programs. Goals include reducing drug use, drug
    trafficking, drug-related crime and violence, and drug-related health
    problems.

Partnership for a Drug-Free America
    405 Lexington Avenue, Suite 1601
    New York, NY 10174
    212-922-1560
    http://www.drugfree.org
    Partnership for a Drug-Free America is a resource for parents trying to
    raise drug-free kids. The organization offers information on drug use
    prevention, addiction, and treatment.

FURTHER READING, WEBSITES, AND FILMS

Balkin, Karen, ed. *Drug Legalization*. Farmington Hills, MI: Greenhaven Press, 2005.
This book gathers essays from newspapers, magazines, books, and government documents. In these writings, various experts give different points of view about the debate over legalized drugs.

Hyde, Margaret O., and John F. Setaro. *Drugs 101: An Overview*. Minneapolis: Twenty-First Century Books, 2003.
Written specifically for teens, this comprehensive title discusses the physical and psychological consequences of drug use, including addiction. The authors also examine the Drug War and the debate over drug legalization.

Karr Editorial. *Drug Abuse*. Farmington Hills, MI: Greenhaven Press, 2007.
Part of the Social Issues Firsthand series, this hard-hitting book includes contributions from teenage drug users, recovering drug addicts, and parents of drug-using teens.

Kuhn, Cynthia, Scott Swartzwelder, and Wilkie Wilson. *Buzzed: The Straight Facts about the Most Used and Abused Drugs, from Alcohol to Ecstasy*. New York: W. W. Norton and Co., 2008.
The authors investigate commonly abused drugs one by one, describing each drug's history, health effects, and risks. They also present general information on addiction, drug laws, and other drug-related topics.

Landau, Elaine. *Meth: America's Drug Epidemic*. Minneapolis: Twenty-First Century Books, 2007.
In this eye-opening title, author Elaine Landau examines the methamphetamine epidemic and how communities and lawmakers are fighting this dangerous drug.

Marcovitz, Hal. *Marijuana*. Farmington Hills, MI: Lucent Books, 2006.
This title examines the history of marijuana use, how marijuana affects the brain and body, the culture surrounding marijuana use, medical marijuana, and the legalization debate.

Parks, Peggy. *Drug Legalization: Current Issues.* San Diego: ReferencePoint Press, 2008.
This title investigates the debate over drug legalization: whether it would reduce crime or increase addiction and whether certain drugs should be legalized and not others.

Roleff, Tamara. *The War on Drugs.* Farmington Hills, MI: Greenhaven Press, 2004.
Every year the United States spends billions of dollars to fight illegal drugs. Is the War on Drugs working? This book examines the issue from many angles.

Sheff, Nic. *Tweak: Growing up on Methamphetamines.* New York: Atheneum, 2009.
In this disturbing memoir, Nic Sheff tells of his teenage descent into drug use and addiction. Nic's father, David Sheff, tells the story from his point of view in his own book *Beautiful Boy*.

WEBSITES

Addiction

http://www.hbo.com/addiction
The website is a companion to a Home Box Office nine-segment film on drug addiction. The site features detailed information on drug addiction and treatment, with specific information on adolescent addiction.

Drug Wars

http://www.pbs.org/wgbh/pages/frontline/shows/drugs/
This site from the Public Broadcasting Service features interviews with physicians and other experts, information on drugs and drug addiction, in-depth reports on the drug trade, and much more.

FILMS

Down to the Bone. DVD. New York: Arts Alliance America, 2006.
This gritty independent film follows the struggles of a young mother as she negotiates drug addiction, rehab, and the drug-enforcement system.

Traffic. DVD. Universal City, CA: Universal Studios, 2002.
This award-winning film dissects the drug trade by interweaving the stories of a variety of characters: the U.S. drug czar, his drug-addicted teenage daughter, Mexican and U.S. drug enforcement agents, and Mexican and U.S. drug traffickers.

The Union: The Business behind Getting High. DVD. Toronto: Peace Arch Home Entertainment, 2007.
This documentary film presents the case for legalizing marijuana. It features interviews with members of Law Enforcement Against Prohibition and other legalization proponents.

INDEX

PHOTO ACKNOWLEDGMENTS

The images in this book are used with the permission of: © Al Bello/Octagon/
Getty Images, pp. 4–5; © Business Wire via Getty Images, p. 6; © Ulf Andersen/
Getty Images, p. 8; © Stapleton Collection/CORBIS, pp. 10–11; © Francois Guenet/
Art Resource, NY, p. 12; © Bob Daemmrich/CORBIS, p. 15; © SSPL/The Image Works,
p. 16; © Hagley Museum and Library, p. 18; © Mary Evans Picture Library/The Image
Works, p. 20; © Time Life Pictures/Mansell/Getty Images, p. 21; Private Collection/
The Stapleton Collection/The Bridgeman Art Library, p. 22; The Art Archive/Culver
Pictures, p. 24; AP Photo, pp. 26–27; © Robert Altman/The Image Works, p. 30;
© Tom Nebbia/CORBIS, p. 33; © Tim Dillon/USA TODAY, pp. 34, 52 (left); 66; AP Photo/
Roberto Borea, p. 36; AP Photo/Efrain Patino, p. 38; © Chris Hawley/USA TODAY, p. 39;
AP Photo/Alexandre Meneghini, File, p. 42; © Mark Wilson/Getty Images, pp. 44–45;
© Jack Kurtz/USA TODAY, p. 46; © Eileen Blass/USA TODAY, p. 49; AP Photo/LM
Otero, p. 50; © M.P.King/USA TODAY, p. 52 (right); © Brendan Fitterer/St. Petersburg
Times/ZUMA Press, p. 53; AP Photo/Jim Cole, p. 54; © Margaret Bourke-White/Time
Life Pictures/Getty Images, p. 56; © SONNY TUMBELAKA/AFP/Getty Images, p. 57;
© Reuters/CORBIS, pp. 59, 85; © Jym Wilson/USA TODAY, p. 60; © Adam Rountree/
Getty Images, pp. 64–65; AP Photo/Toby Talbot, p. 69; © John Olson/Time Life
Pictures/Getty Images, p. 71; AP Photo/York Daily Record, Paul Kuehnel, p. 72; © Scott
Olson/Getty Images, p. 75; © Tim Boyle/Getty Images, pp. 78–79; © Chris Jackson/
IMPictures/FilmMagic/Getty Images, p. 81 (left); © Alexander Tamargo/Getty Images,
p. 81 (right); © Annie Griffiths Belt/CORBIS, p. 82; © Wm. Baker/GhostWorx Images/
Alamy, p. 86; © Chicago History Museum/Hulton Archive/Getty Images, p. 87; © Alex
Wong/Newsmakers/Getty Images, p. 89; © J. Guadalupe PEREZ/AFP/Getty Images,
p. 91; © Shawn Ehlers/WireImage/Getty Images, p. 93; © Gene Sloan/USA TODAY,
p. 95; © Adisa/Dreamstime.com, p. 98; © Samuel Wordley/Alamy, pp. 100–101;
© David McNew/Getty Images, p. 103; AP Photo/CP, Stephen Thorne, p. 104; © David
Sutherland/Photographer's Choice/Getty Images, p. 107; © Wolpert Wolpert/
F1 Online/Photolibrary, pp. 112–113; © Yong hian Lim/Dreamstime.com, p. 117;
© Robin Weiner/USA TODAY, pp. 121, 130; © Justin Sullivan/Getty Images, pp. 123,
126; © James Keyser/Time Life Pictures/Getty Images, p. 128; © Frances Roberts/
Alamy, pp. 132–133; © iStockphoto.com/Chris Schmidt, p. 135; AP Photo/Journal
Times, Mark Hertzberg, p. 136; © Alex Wong/Getty Images, p. 138; © H. Darr Beiser/
USA TODAY, p. 140.

Cover: © Chris Cheadle/All Canada Photos/Getty Images.

ABOUT THE AUTHOR

Margaret J. Goldstein was born in Detroit and graduated from the University of
Michigan. She is an editor and author for young readers. She lives in Santa Fe,
New Mexico.